DAMON HILL

THE QUEST FOR SPEED
Modern racing car design and technology

DRIVING FORCES
Fifty men who shaped the world of motor racing

WILLIAMS
The business of Grand Prix racing

FIFTY FAMOUS MOTOR RACES

DEREK BELL
My racing life

FERRARI
The Grand Prix Cars

BRABHAM
The Grand Prix cars

MARCH
The Grand Prix and Indy cars

JACKIE STEWART'S PRINCIPLES OF PERFORMANCE DRIVING

Patrick Stephens Limited, an imprint of Haynes Publishing, has published authoritative, quality books for enthusiasts for more than 25 years. During that time the company has established a reputation as one of the world's leading publishers of books on aviation, maritime, military, model-making, motor cycling, motoring, motor racing, railway and railway modelling subjects. Readers or authors with suggestions for books they would like to see published are invited to write to: The Editorial Director, Patrick Stephens Limited, Sparkford, Nr. Yeovil, Somerset BA22 7JJ.

DAMON HILL

FROM ZERO TO HERO

ALAN HENRY

Patrick Stephens Limited

First published in 1994

British Library cataloguing-in-publication data:
A catalogue record for this book is
available from the British Library.

ISBN: 1 85260 484 0

Library of Congress catalog card no: 93 81191

Patrick Stephens Limited is an imprint of Haynes Publishing,
Sparkford, Nr. Yeovil, Somerset BA22 7JJ.

Typeset by G&M, Raunds, Northamptonshire.
Printed in Great Britain by Butler & Tanner Ltd, London and Frome.

Contents

Acknowledgements

I WOULD PARTICULARLY like to thank Peter Foubister, Publisher of *Autosport*, and David Tremayne, Executive Editor of *Motoring News*, for permission to quote from their respective publications which, between them, represent what amount to on-going, weekly standard works of reference for the motor racing historian. Also to Johnny Herbert, Martin Donnelly and Mark Blundell, for their recollections of racing with Damon. Other reflections came from Bette Hill, Dan Gurney, Ray Boulter, Patrick Head, Frank Williams, Peter Collins and John Wickham, for which I am equally grateful. Thanks also to Steve Tee and Kathy Agar of LAT Photographic, to Ann Bradshaw, Richard West and Jane Gorard of Williams Grand Prix Engineering, Peter Weale, Tim Bampton and Caroline O'Connor of Brands Hatch and *Motorcycle News*.

• CHAPTER ONE •

Son of a famous father

THE LOCALS IN Budapest admitted that they were hard pressed to recall August weather like it. The temperature was nudging 100° Fahrenheit beneath a clear blue sky as a dazzling, multi-coloured array of 24 Formula 1 cars prepared to set out on their parade lap at the start of the 1993 Hungarian Grand Prix.

Yet, when the flag was waved to send them on their way, only 23 of those competitors moved away on cue. Sitting proudly on pole position, the dark blue, bright yellow and white Williams-Renault No. 2 remained rooted to the spot. Strapped deep in its cockpit, triple World Champion Alain Prost cursed his luck. He had stalled his engine.

Now the Frenchman, at 38 a veteran of 12 years in front-line F1 and the all-time most successful exponent of this demanding sport, could effectively kiss goodbye to any prospect of adding to his record 51 Grand Prix victories. On that afternoon, at least.

After an agonizing few seconds, his Renault V10 engine was eventually coaxed into life with the assistance of his mechanics, and he chased off after the pack. But the rules clearly stated that he would now have to start at the back of the field.

For the driver of the other Williams, this was a bonus of incalculable proportions. Now Damon Hill would not have to race his illustrious team-mate. If he kept his head, the first-ever victory, in the

7

44-season history of the official World Championship, for a second generation member of a Grand Prix winning family, would be his.

One hour, forty seven minutes, thirty nine-point-zero-nine-eight seconds later, Damon Hill accelerated his Williams-Renault FW15C past the chequered flag to realize that dreamlike ambition.

He finished the race over a minute ahead of the Benetton of Riccardo Patrese, the man whom he had succeeded in the second Williams seat at the start of the year. For much of the race Damon had run alone, under no immediate pressure. The real pressure – not to make a mistake, not to throw it all away – had come from within.

'I kept telling myself it's not over until it's over,' he said reflectively at the post race conference, 'and I thought of my dad and what he might have said to me to keep my concentration up. And if you knew my dad, you know that just imagining him talking to me was enough to make me concentrate!' It was a remark which brought a quiet smile to the faces of many journalistic old timers.

The obvious sub-text to Damon's remark was left unspoken; that his 'Old Man' would have been bursting with pride had he been around to share that historic day.

Truth be told, it was the helmet colours that did it. If Damon Hill had ever hoped to escape from the shadow of his legendary father, it was ironic that he took a decisive step early in his career which would ensure his own identity would be inextricably, permanently linked with Graham's reputation and image.

It would not matter that he was to carve his own outstanding niche in contemporary Grand Prix racing history, winning a hat trick of races in his first full F1 season.

No matter that he successfully filled the vacuum caused by reigning World Champion Nigel Mansell's defection to Indycars in 1993.

No matter that, in 12 months, he became possibly as big a media star as his father had managed in almost two decades of motor racing. As long as he wore that helmet, Damon Hill would remain a hostage to his long-dead father's memory.

From his debut in motor racing, Damon opted to display the dark blue helmet livery with the white vertical stripes, the colours of the London Rowing Club of which his father had been an enthusiastic member in the early 1950s. Born in a Hampstead nursing home on 15

Following in father's footsteps. Damon takes the microphone after his historic maiden F1 victory in the 1993 Hungarian Grand Prix at Budapest. Riccardo Patrese (right) finished second ahead of Gerhard Berger (left).

February, 1929, there was nothing about Graham Hill's background or upbringing to suggest he would ever scale any great heights of personal achievement.

Yet the moustachioed Londoner, who never drove a car of any sort until he was 24, made up for lost time in epic fashion to carve himself a career as one of Britain's most successful Grand Prix drivers. More than that, he drove into the hearts of the British public as a national hero.

Graham was right up there with the likes of Henry Cooper, Bobby Charlton and Colin Cowdrey in the mind of the man in the street. He was perceived as a genuine Sporting Gladiator at a time when such personalities were held in awe as much for the flawless manner in which they conducted themselves under the spotlight of public attention as for what they achieved in their chosen field.

He won two World Championships, 14 Grands Prix, Le Mans and the Indianapolis 500 before retiring mid-way through the 1975 season after competing in a then-record 176 Grands Prix.

When Graham Hill was killed in an air crash, on a foggy, depressing Sunday evening in November that same year, the nation's heart missed a beat. For this wasn't one of today's highly paid, obsessively professional and secretive sporting technocrats; this was a gregarious, outgoing, extrovert character equally at home on a television chat show as strapped into the confines of a Grand Prix cockpit.

He could converse with royalty or ruffian alike with an easy, relaxed charm. He was a man's man and, with the halcyon days of his Formula 1 ascendency played out through the socially liberating 1960s, he became one of professional sport's first genuine media personalities.

There was nothing dour or introverted about Graham Hill. Blessed with a dry wit and a quick thinking mind, he was adored from afar by legions of fans who had only a passing interest in the sport of motor racing.

The well-timed saucy wink, the mane of dark hair and the well-trimmed moustache all added up to an image of the classic, congenial Englishman sallying forth to do battle on behalf of his country against those marauding hordes of 'Foreign Johnnies' who, it went without saying, were distinctly suspect, as we were recently reminded by Mr Michael Portillo, MP!

Graham had first sampled a racing car in late 1953, paying £1 for four laps of Brands Hatch at the wheel of an ancient 500cc F3 car. He found it very much to his taste. However, his ambitions to swap a career working for Smiths Industries for motor racing stardom would initially be thwarted by a crucial, tangential consideration – namely, lack of cash.

Nevertheless, thanks to a well-executed programme of socializing and sheer hard work, Graham got a job as a mechanic with Colin Chapman's fledgeling Lotus team, a key move which eventually led to his F1 debut with the team at Monaco in 1958.

It was Graham's transfer to the BRM team which really set him on the road towards serious success at the start of the 1960 season. Moreover, by the time he led that year's British Grand Prix at Silverstone, only to spin off under pressure from Jack Brabham's winning Cooper in the closing stages, his wife Bette was heavily pregnant with the second of their three children.

On 17 September Bette gave birth to their only son. Graham wasn't present for the great event as he was away racing at Snetterton, in Norfolk, in company with his famous contemporaries Jo Bonnier and Dan Gurney.

Taking it all in his stride: Six-year-old Damon yawns as he sits with his father on the pit counter at Monza during the 1967 Italian Grand Prix weekend. Graham drove a works Lotus 49 in the race; leading but failing to finish.

In his autobiography, *Life at the Limit* (William Kimber, 1969; republished by Patrick Stephens Limited, 1993) Graham recalled: 'Bette rang me at 8.30 a.m. on the morning of the race to tell me I was the father of a son and I was naturally delighted. She says that my first reaction was to ask if that was all she'd woken me up to tell me, but I don't think I was quite as callous as that . . . The morning after the race, I went straight to the hospital to visit Bette and our new baby boy.'

A few weeks later, the Hill son and heir was duly christened Damon Graham Devereux at St Paul's Church, Mill Hill, close to number 12 Parkside, the family's comfortable, if unpretentious detached home in that north London enclave. Shortly afterwards, Graham would depart to compete in the Portuguese Grand Prix for the BRM team.

Throughout Damon's childhood, Graham Hill was away for a very great deal of the time. In those days, not only did top-line international racing drivers compete in a full programme of World Championship Grands Prix, but there were many non-title F1 races, touring car and sports car events and, later, the Indianapolis 500 which Graham would win in 1966 at his first attempt.

In the meantime, he would win the 1962 World Championship at the wheel of a BRM and establish a reputation as second only to Jim Clark in the perceived international F1 pecking order. From a family viewpoint, there seems little doubt that Graham Hill was a traditional, warm-hearted and generous father, even if he was apparently wedded to the principle that the man provides and the woman waits.

His critics branded him selfish and self-absorbed. Certainly, the sheer inner steel which helped Graham drag himself up by his bootstraps from his background of suburban anonymity to achieve international fame and fortune had a less appealing spin-off in terms of a stormy side to his personality.

He could be crushingly, dismissively rude if the mood took him, and even those close to him found that they were not always immune from verbal lashings, some of which were – unforgiveably – conducted in front of an audience. Yet such intolerance was not once put on show to his adoring public. For them, the mask never slipped.

For the most part, Damon and his sisters Brigitte and Samantha have affectionate recollections of those early days. Brigitte Hill has perceptively put her finger on the warm and comfortable atmosphere which prevailed at the family's home in Mill Hill as she grew up. In the revised new edition of *Life at the Limit* (Patrick Stephens Limited, 1993) she says:

> The sixties for us – the height of Daddy's career – was a whirl of parties, tons of people at the house, Mummy and Daddy going away and coming back again (our grandmother's cine films consisted almost entirely of us leaving our home at Mill Hill and then returning), interspersed with school, piano lessons, *Doctor Who*, Honey our retriever, and summer days playing in the street with our friends at Parkside. A normal childhood, we thought, and in many ways it was.

After winning the 1962 World Championship, for the next few years Hill and BRM became identified as one. Graham achieved a hat trick of victories at Monaco between 1963 and 1965, just failing to win the 1964 championship after being knocked out of the season's finale in

Mexico by the wayward Lorenzo Bandini's Ferrari.

He was joined in the BRM squad by promising rising star Jackie Stewart in 1965. It is possible that Graham felt somewhat upstaged by the chirpy Scot, with the result that he caused a sensation in F1 circles by rejoining Lotus for 1967, partnering his old rival Jimmy Clark. Ford had bankrolled the development of the brand new Cosworth-built DFV V8 which was to power Chapman's sensational new challenger, the Lotus 49, and it only made sense to recruit the strongest possible driving team available.

However, by the start of the 1968 season, Graham found himself cast increasingly in a supporting role to Clark, who scored a record 25th career victory in the first race of the season, the South African Grand Prix. Barely three months later, the burden of team leadership came slamming down onto Graham's shoulders when Jimmy was killed in an inconsequential, minor-league F2 race at Hockenheim.

Graham . . . steadied the troops and restored morale . . . winning the 1968 Championship

It is no exaggeration to say that Graham proved an emotional rock on which the trembling Team Lotus could lean in the shell-shocked aftermath of Clark's death. Colin Chapman briefly, seriously, considered giving up racing altogether. But Graham, by now almost staring his 40th birthday in the face, steadied the troops and restored morale by picking up Clark's gauntlet and winning the 1968 World Championship.

The following Spring he would win for the fifth time at Monaco. This was a record which would not be surpassed until Senna beat Damon into second place through the streets of the Mediterranean Principality a quarter of a century later. But it was also Graham Hill's final Grand Prix victory.

At the end of the season he would sustain fearful leg injuries when he was flung from his car in an accident during the United States GP at Watkins Glen.

Refusing to be written off, he forced the pace of his recovery in a manner which was truly awesome in order to be ready for the start of the 1970 season. Yet Colin Chapman – with characteristic cold and

Halcyon days. Graham Hill at the absolute zenith of his achievement, carrying number one on his BRM to signify he is reigning World Champion as he speeds to third place in the 1963 British Grand Prix at Silverstone.

unemotional pragmatism – could see that Graham was now a spent force as far as F1 was concerned, and successfully shunted him off into the private team run by the highly respected Rob Walker.

The end of the decade marked the finish of Graham Hill's career as an effective Grand Prix force. After a painfully unsuccessful season with the Walker Lotus, he switched to Brabham in 1971 for whom he won the non-title Silverstone International Trophy. By 1973, with sponsorship from the Embassy cigarette brand, he had founded his own team.

Driving a Shadow DN1, Graham's progress amounted to an excruciating embarrassment for those who recalled his Grand Prix heyday. In 1974 the team switched to Lola chassis, then in 1975 established itself as a constructor. Graham finally took the long overdue decision to stand down from the cockpit after failing to qualify at Monaco, his beloved stamping ground.

Yet there was light flickering on the horizon. Graham now concentrated his efforts on furthering the career of Tony Brise, one of the most talented rising stars thrown up by the British domestic motor racing academy. For 1976 the plan was for Hill to field a single car team for the gifted newcomer. Tragically, these best laid plans never came to fruition.

On 29 November, 1975 Graham took off from the airstrip adjoining the Paul Ricard circuit, near Bandol in southern France, after a troubled test session with the latest Hill GH2 F1 challenger. With him in the six-seater Piper Aztec aircraft, bought in the USA out of his 1965 Indy 500 winnings, were Brise, designer Andy Smallman, team manager Ray Brimble and two mechanics, Tony Alcock and Terry Richards.

The weather may have been clear for their departure from the Cote d'Azur, but much of southern England was shrouded in freezing fog, although Graham remained confident he would be able to land at Elstree, his home base. Rejecting suggestions that he divert to Luton, where additional navigation aids were available, he pressed on with his original flight plan.

Barely five miles from its planned touch-down, the Aztec cartwheeled to fiery destruction on Arkley golf course, killing all its occupants. A glorious chapter in Britain's post-war motor racing history had abruptly come to an end.

Double Zero. Damon wasn't the first Hill to race with zero in 1993. Thirty years earlier, Graham and his BRM team-mate Richie Ginther carried this identification on the Rover-BRM gas turbine car in the Le Mans 24-hour sports car classic.

Yet, even in their grief, fate had yet to deal another cruel hand to Graham Hill's family. The insurance company would not pay out because Graham had overlooked renewing his pilot's licence, and the bereaved families had no alternative to the painful course of suing his estate to obtain financial compensation. In short, Graham's estate was cleaned out.

Bette and the family suddenly found themselves having to move from Lyndhurst, their magnificent 25-room country mansion at Shenley, deep in the Hertfordshire countryside, to a modest semi-detached property in St Albans. It was a devasting blow, yet an ample helping of Graham's grit and singlemindedness had obviously rubbed off on his family. Uncomplainingly, they settled down to make the best of their new circumstances.

To this day, Damon remains philosophical about life's twists and turns. As if the loss of his father wasn't enough, he and his wife Georgie have since had to cope with the challenge of a Downs syndrome child. Surmounting these hurdles has helped him to develop a pleasantly well-rounded, if rather reserved, character.

'Rather than dwell on all the detail of it, I think I can sum it all up by saying that perhaps I'm a bit more experienced (about life) than some of my contemporaries,' he says modestly.

'I thought, well I've been very privileged for the first 15 years of my life, but now I'm going to have to get on with it like Dad did. He started from scratch and made his own way. Now I had to do the same.'

Damon admits that he has learned not to try rationalizing the tragedy of his father's death.

'What's the reasoning behind a guy doing one of the most dangerous sports, throughout one of the most dangerous periods in the 1960s and early '70s, then retiring and dying in a plane crash,' he muses thoughtfully.

Losing a parent can have a devastating long-term effect on an adolescent

'You tend to think about that for a long time, wondering what's the reason for it. But you come to the conclusion that there's no reason behind it and, if you try to rationalize it, then you drive yourself round the bend. To think that you are owed anything in life is wrong. It's not like that.

'My father had a code of conduct, a certain belief. He wasn't somebody who wanted to be seen to be complaining about things. He took the rough with the smooth – took it like a man, if you like. That was definitely something he tried to impart to me. Not directly, but by example.'

It must be seen as a tribute to Bette Hill's solid common sense and practicality that Damon, Brigitte and Samantha all grew up into level-headed and responsible adults. Losing a parent is a traumatic experience at any age, but it can have a devastating long-term effect on an adolescent. Damon was inching his way to a mature, mutually enriching relationship with his father when Graham was killed.

As things are, Damon has comfortable, albeit distant, memories of his father as an attentive, if frequently absent parent. Early in 1993, he told Nick Pitt of *The Times*: 'He died when I was 14. I wish people would tell me more about him because I only have a very sketchy memory of what he was like.

'I was just getting to know him. I never seemed to spend much time with him at home, he seemed to be away a hell of a lot. I never saw the real Graham Hill, the gregarious kind of hell-raiser that people talk about, because I think he kept himself in check when he was around the children.

'He was in the Royal Navy as a Chief Petty Officer, then he joined the London Rowing Club and there are pictures of him at the Henley Regatta with stripey blazer and cap, and a handlebar moustache – it was even bigger in those days, a bushy, twirling thing. He was a cross between David Niven and Terry Thomas, one of those types, and I'm sure he played up to that character. If anybody has got any tapes of him doing an after-dinner speech anywhere, I'd like to get them, I'd love to hear his speeches.

'Having children of my own is like an echo of him. I can remember what it was like when I was young. I come back now and they are in bed and I tuck them up, and I can remember my father coming home, always coming home late, but always coming in to kiss me goodnight. I remember how nice that was. When I see my children I remember the things I enjoyed about my father, climbing all over him, jumping up and down on him.'

Later, he told the author: 'It's true he spent a lot of time away. But when he was at home he very much liked to be with his family, although you always got the slight feeling that he wasn't quite there, even though he was present!

'Georgie is always prodding me when I'm home to listen to what the children are saying. I'm very conscious of that because I've been through it with my father. He might have been around, but I feel that he wasn't the type who was always giving it his full attention.

'He was too involved with his cars, or whatever, but I don't know whether you can get to the top in any profession without giving it 100 per cent effort and attention. The only thing I can say is that I am aware of the danger of that factor. I make sure I attend to my children when I am at home.'

His observations reveal that Graham had got to the point that he was treating Damon like a young adult, genuinely caring what the boy felt about his decisions.

'At the time he was killed, I was just beginning to have more of an interest in his team,' admits Damon. 'Who knows, if he had lived, the

Graham Hill was at ease amongst fellow celebrities – here with comedian Bruce Forsyth at Brands Hatch in 1974.

Graham (third from right) at a Ford promotional day in 1973 in the company of (from left to right), RAF hero Douglas Bader, yachstman Chay Blyth, three day eventer Richard Meade, boxer Henry Cooper and cricket legend Colin Cowdrey. Hill senior absolutely excelled at such PR operations.

Hill team might well be where Williams is now.' It would have been a tantalizing possibility. Either way, Graham and Damon were beginning to do things together, most notably fooling around on motorcycle scramble bikes through the spacious grounds of Lyndhurst.

Common ground between father and son during adolescence can be difficult to find. If it is, it can be enormously rewarding. As Keke Rosberg, the 1982 World Champion remembers affectionately of his father: 'During my early teens he supported me when I wanted to go karting and was always coming along with me. I'm absolutely certain that it strengthened our relationship and prevented all the father-and-son tensions from developing. Thanks to him, I breezed through my teenage years without any of those problems.'

Damon was now deprived of this opportunity for personal bonding. To be honest, however, years of exposure to motor racing had caused him to become disinterested with the sport. He rather took his father's job for granted. Some kids had a father who worked in the bank, Damon had a father who drove racing cars. That was his job, rationalized the uncomplicated child's mind. It was all very logical.

Even Graham's five victories at Monaco were as water off a duck's back to Damon. He recalls the afternoon of his father's final victory through the streets of the Principality, during the spring of 1969 – that final Grand Prix victory of his career.

'The only thing I remember about him in connection with Monaco was when we were staying at a friend's cottage in Kent,' says Damon. 'I was playing in the garden with their son, Nick, and Mum came out and said, 'Come and look at Daddy winning the Monaco Grand Prix,' and I sort of thought, 'Can't I stay out here and play?'

'I must have been eight years old at the time and I remember coming in and watching Dad coming round the old Gasworks hairpin in the red and gold Lotus 49 and sort of finishing the race, and that was it. It didn't impress me at all.'

Added weight is given to Damon's take-it-for-granted approach to his father's celebrity status by an occasion when he turned to Bette and said, 'Mummy, who can I ask for an autograph?' He wanted somebody else's because he regarded his father's as a bit commonplace. Also, he hardly ever referred to his father's profession when he was at school. Much to the frustration of his classmates, one can safely assume!

Career twilight. Graham struggling with the Shadow-Ford DN1 which was the main-stay of his Embassy-sponsored F1 team during its disappointing fledgeling season in 1973.

Left *A new chapter opens. Damon with mother Bette at Brands Hatch, poised between two wheels and four!*

'I never came to Monaco with my father, but I remember growing up thinking that winning the Monaco Grand Prix was his job. That was what we did for a living. We used to go to the Italian Grand Prix quite regularly, combining it with family holidays; but not to Monaco.'

In the aftermath of Graham's death, Bette insisted that Damon took his A-level examinations, and then enrolled him at the South Bank Polytechnic to do business studies. As things turned out, he didn't complete the course, and his increasing obsession with motor cycles would steer him towards racing on two wheels when, in the early days, he would keep body and soul together working as a despatch rider.

For the record, Damon was also once a member of a punk band known as – wait for it – Sex Hitler and the Hormones! Not quite the image of a clean-cut, future Grand Prix driver, perhaps, but then youth always brings with it some little foibles!

Two years after Graham's death, Bette wrote her own touching memoirs entitled *The Other Side of the Hill*. Of the teenaged Damon, she noted:

Soon after we'd moved out to St Albans he went out on his moped, then came home. As he had kept his helmet on, I said, 'Where are you going?'

'I'm going out,' he said as he lifted the visor and pushed his face forward to kiss me. It took my breath away – his face and everything about him was so like Graham.

The helmet probably helped to provide a familiar frame to the picture, but the face inside it was so like Graham's, and so were the mannerisms. When I used to ask Graham where he was going, that's just what he said: 'I'm going out.'

• CHAPTER TWO •

On two wheels and four

DAMON HILL WAS talking during a test session at Silverstone in late June, 1993. It was a few weeks short of 12 months since he'd made his Grand Prix debut, at the wheel of an arthritic Brabham-Judd, at the same circuit. He started last and finished in the same position, 16th overall and four laps behind Nigel Mansell's victorious Williams-Renault FW14B into which Damon had put so many hours of development testing.

He was only a couple of weeks away from tackling the same event at the wheel of his own Williams-Renault FW15C. His father had never won the British Grand Prix in 16 years of trying. Now Damon was hoping to make up for that omission.

'Certainly, Silverstone has a lot of memories,' he said reflectively. 'We used to fly in with Dad's plane – and in those days, having a twin-prop aircraft was a big thing. To fly into the circuit here was a traditional day out for us.'

Ironically, it was also at Silverstone where young Damon's head was turned away from racing cars almost for good. The occasion was the 1971 International Trophy race, a two-heat non-championship

Right *Making his own way. Damon, celebrating one of his many two-wheeled victories at Brands Hatch, waves to the crowd on his lap of honour.*

race which traditionally served as a key warm-up for the start of the European leg of the World Championship.

Father Graham was in fine form and, more through stealth and measured judgement than outstanding pace, emerged victorious at the wheel of the distinctive Brabham BT34.

Yet, proud though Damon was of his father's achievements, by the time the race began his thoughts were firmly planted elsewhere. He'd first driven a car at the age of five and would later crash around in a battered old Austin A40 ('It had been Graham's car, his mother's car, his brother's car, my car – everybody's car,' recalled Bette) but it was to life on two wheels that he now became magnetically attracted.

Somebody had been riding around the Silverstone paddock on a tiny 50cc monkey bike, and Damon was absolutely hypnotized with fascination. From then on, motorcycles were absolutely at the forefront of Hill junior's mind.

'. . . I was really excited about seeing those guys riding the bikes'

'This guy let me have a go, and I thought, "This is fantastic, this is what I want to do. I want one of these,"' recalls Damon with absolute clarity.

'So I said to my dad sheepishly, "What do you think the chances are?" and he got me one for passing my Eleven-Plus examination. I was absolutely stunned. I thought it was the best thing that had happened in my life. I've still got it and, from that moment on, I was into bikes. I used to get every bike magazine I could find – about moto-cross, circuit racing . . . anything.

'After I developed that initial interest, Dad got into bikes himself because we had some land (at Shenley) on which we could ride. He got a 350cc trials bike off Bultaco, the Spanish maker, which he used to ride round enthusiastically.

'Obviously that was a lot more powerful than my 50cc monkey bike and I was a bit surprised that he let me have a go. But he just told me to wear my helmet and be careful! After that, I just wasn't interested in the 50cc bike anymore. That was the moment, I think, that I discovered speed and power.'

After his father's death, Damon remembers being taken down to Brands Hatch for the Trans-Atlantic trophy motorcycle race by Peter Gethin, who was latterly a contemporary of his father in F1.

'After years of having seen Grand Prix and saloon car races – which did absolutely nothing for me – I found I was really excited about seeing those guys riding the bikes,' he reflected. 'I can't explain it, but I knew I really wanted to have a go at that.'

Interestingly Gethin, who earned his place in the F1 record books by winning the 1971 Italian Grand Prix at a then-record average speed of 150 mph, and, by coincidence, had his last ever Grand Prix outing in Graham's second Embassy Hill at Brands Hatch in 1974, has no recollection of taking Damon on that day out.

'That's not to say it didn't happen,' said Peter in 1994, 'but I just can't recall it. I do remember young Damon crashing about on his father's trials bikes around the grounds at Shenley, though. I remember thinking he was a very pleasant young fellow – very much like Bette rather than Graham as far as his personality was concerned, I have always thought.'

Damon started bike racing in 1981 on a Kawasaki. He used to ride from St Albans all the way to south London to help a friend who was working in the building trade, gutting houses in preparation for restoration. All the money so earned went into his motorcycle racing kitty.

'I used to finish putting the bike together at nine o'clock in the evening, borrow my Mum's car, hitch up the trailer and drive up north,' he recalls. 'I'd arrive at the track at about one in the morning, pitch my tent, get up at seven because of the cold, then try to qualify and race. More often than not, I was so knackered that I fell off.'

At the end of 1983, Brands Hatch supremo John Webb organized him some outings in an Argo JM16 Formula Ford car for the end-of-season BBC Grandstand series at the Kent circuit. It proved to be a mixed experience.

As one Formula 3 team owner recalled to *Motoring News*: 'I felt sorry for the kid. He just didn't seem to have a clue what he was doing.'

Damon broadly concurs, admitting that the switch to cars 'was a total culture shock. All of a sudden, I had to fiddle with the vehicle rather than simply trying harder to go faster. It was no longer a matter

Main picture *Damon leans into Druids hairpin at Brands Hatch during his motorcycling days – his face etched with the expression his mother found so strikingly reminiscent of Graham.*

Inset *With fellow rider Ioni Holmes, pondering the Yamaha TZ350, again at Brands Hatch.*

of getting good tyres and checking that the chain wasn't loose – and the cornering was so much faster!'

Perhaps a little disheartened, he went back to bikes for 1984 and scored more than 40 race wins, riding both a Yamaha TZ 350 in the Champion of Brands series and an LC350 in the national Pro-Am series where he found himself stacked up against the likes of Neil Mackenzie and the late Kenny Irons.

'He wasn't a slow rider, but, to be frank, he didn't really look destined for great things,' says Rob McDonnell, the Road Race GP reporter for *Motorcycle News*. Yet Damon was still operating on a shoestring working out of a garage rented by car racer Barrie Williams and a £50 Transit van.

He seems pretty satisfied with what he achieved. 'There's more a rider can do on a bike,' he insists. 'He's much more a percentage of the package than the bike itself.'

In 1983 he had attended the Winfield Racing School at the old Magny-Cours circuit where he had displayed above-average aptitude. Bette was the one who encouraged him to take this course. 'He was very good on them [bikes], but they were so dangerous they scared me. I thought he would be safer in a car,' she said.

He switched back to cars towards the end of 1984, winning his first Formula Ford race at Brands Hatch in August. He picked up a Special Commendation in the end-of-season Grovewood Awards after only half a season of racing, and began to gear up for a full season of car racing in 1985.

With backing from Ricoh, the office equipment supplies company, Damon organized a full programme of major-league domestic Formula Ford races, driving for the Manadient Racing Team run by Kevin Barrett.

At the wheel of a Van Diemen RF85, he was now seriously jousting against others who would join him as Grand Prix stars in the future – and others who hoped they might make the grade. He raced alongside Mark Blundell, man-to-beat Johnny Herbert and Bertrand Gachot. There was also the equally promising crop of talent for whom the cards would never quite fall as favourably as they might

Right *Hanging on to the Yamaha at Brands Hatch – the vertical stripes of the London Rowing Club picked out on the back of his leathers as well as on his helmet.*

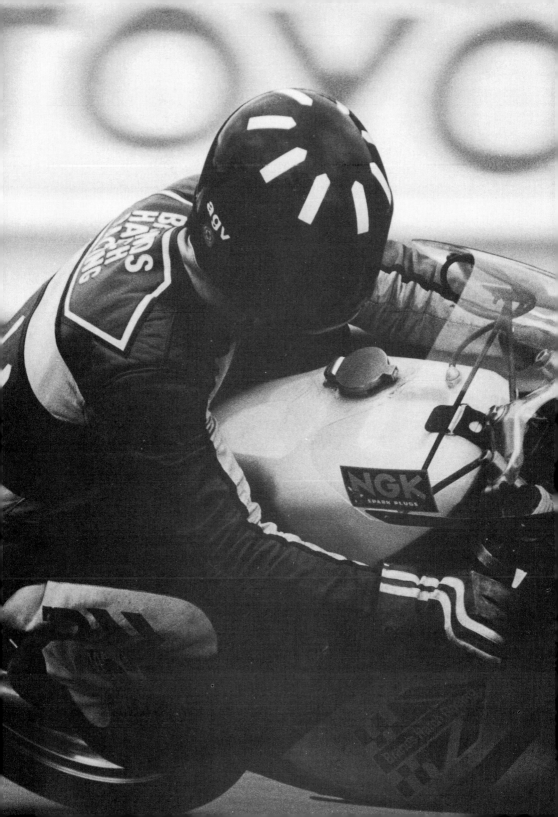

Main picture *Damon lines the Van Diemen up for Bottom Bend on one of his many outings at Brands Hatch during 1984.*

Inset *In the middle of the front row at Brands Hatch with the Manadient Racing Van Diemen FF1600 during his first full season of four-wheeled competition.*

have done – Perry McCarthy, Jonathan Bancroft and Paul Carcasci.

Damon proved quick and unquestionably audacious. The bottom line was that he won six races during the course of the season, finishing third in the Esso FF1600 and fifth in the Townsend Thoresen Championships.

There were also a handful of less memorable, albeit significantly more spectacular moments. Most notable amongst these was an episode at Oulton Park when Damon crashed heavily at the Knicker Brook corner, putting himself in hospital overnight with concussion.

However, he rounded off the season with a fine showing in the cut-and-thrust of the 38-car annual Formula Ford Festival at Brands Hatch where drivers compete both in their own right, and as members of three-car national teams.

Damon won both his heat and the semi-final before going on to take third in the final. His efforts, together with those of Bancroft and Blundell, helped Britain bag the team prize!

More significantly, in the summer of 1985, Damon tested an F3 Ralt-Toyota owned by the Eddie Jordan team at Donington Park. He

Looking thoughtful in the back of the garage – the shroud over the engine cover looks particularly ominous.

turned in some respectable laps, and the outing represented an understandable pointer as to the direction in which he wished to go for 1985. His best lap was half a second away from that set by F3 regular Mauricio Gugelmin's similar machine.

The British Formula 3 championship has, for 30 years now, represented an enormously significant marshalling area for future Grand Prix talent. Formula Ford teaches the bright-eyed hopeful how to race in close company, how to jostle for position and keep his nerve. But F3 takes the learning process one step further.

The apprentice racer now finds himself swapping grooved race tyres for treadless dry weather slicks and also has to come to grips with the intricacies in adjusting wings and front flaps, all of which have a crucial influence on the aerodynamic performance of his new mount.

The most celebrated graduate of the British F3 academy in the last two decades was surely Ayrton Senna, the brilliant Brazilian who went on to become Damon's team-mate in the 1994 Rothmans Williams Renault line-up. Senna had won the 1983 title driving for the West Surrey Racing team run by highly respected F3 operator Dick Bennetts and, ironically, it was to Bennetts' door that Hill beat a path whilst laying plans for his graduation at the start of 1986.

Ricoh was originally planning to stay aboard as his major sponsor and the plan was that Hill would partner Canadian rising star Bertrand Fabi in the two-car West Surrey squad. Disappointingly, the deal fell apart when Ricoh decided to pull out. He thought he had another backer, Warmastyle, on the hook until they decided they would opt to support the national 'Racing for Britain' campaign instead. Damon was offered a contribution to his budget from RFB but, perhaps rashly, he declined.

'Ricoh pulled out just before Christmas and, without exaggeration, I didn't leave the phone or office,' he told David Tremayne of *Motoring News*, the weekly motorsporting newspaper.

'I was there Christmas Day and Boxing Day, putting calls through to the most ridiculous people – some really obscure ones! – just to find something; anything. I was absolutely desperate!

'Commercial deals don't just happen, and just after the Warmastyle deal deflated came the problem with the Racing for Britain money. In retrospect, that was the biggest mistake turning down what was offered there.

Main picture *Hurling the Van Diemen through Paddock Bend, Damon strives to keep ahead of an FF1600 rival.*

Inset *Brands Hatch commentator Brian Jones gives Damon a grilling on the victory rostrum.*

'The way I saw things, I just had to be racing. I'd been reading one of Niki Lauda's books and I figured that if I was really convinced I could do it, I would take a gamble and let things sort themselves out. I borrowed a huge sum on the understanding that it would be paid back, and that is exactly what it will be.

'I decided I would still go for it, but . . . I'd do it to the fullest, not half-heartedly!'

'Money still has a fixed value as far as I am concerned. I did the deal with Dick and everything was set again; we'd bought time to find the money to repay the loan.'

Tragically, the plans became derailed once more. Bertrand Fabi was killed in a horrifyingly violent testing accident at Goodwood, and Bennetts went cold on the idea of another F3 programme for the time being. He decided to switch to Formula 3000 instead, so that left Damon looking for another berth.

'I could have said "forget it" after Bert's death,' Damon admits. 'Dick went through the same thing – everybody involved questioned the whole reason for racing. The darker side of the sport is thankfully rare, but I'd seen it before.

'I remember Dad coming home one day very, very quiet and saw the news film of Jim Clark's death, but I wasn't too sure what it all meant. I was only eight.

'When Bert was killed, I took the conscious decision that I wasn't going to stop doing that sort of thing. It's not just competing; it's doing something exciting. I'm at my fullest skiing, racing, or whatever. And I'm more frightened of letting it all slip and reaching 60 and finding that I've done nothing.

'I was in for a penny and I'd been in for £100,000. I decided I would still go for it, but, most crucial of all, I'd do it to the fullest, not half-heartedly!'

Having borrowed the money necessary to make the graduation, he signed with the Silverstone-based team run by Kiwi Murray Taylor, a former journalist who for many years had been a colleague of the author on the staff of *Motoring News*.

· CHAPTER THREE ·

Onto the professional ladder

THERE WAS MUCH speculation on where the finance came from for Damon's first F3 season. At the time there were rumours that long-time family friend John Coombs, the famous former Guildford-based Jaguar dealer for whom Graham Hill had raced in the early 1960s and who was godfather to Damon's sister Samantha, had helped. Coombs, now retired to Monte Carlo, has made no comment on the matter.

Since starting his F3 team in 1980, Taylor had built up a reputation for fielding well-prepared and dependable cars. Outsiders rated him probably third in terms of overall competence at the time, behind only the West Surrey and Eddie Jordan teams. It was certainly good enough to put Damon in with a decent chance in his freshman year.

Damon's team-mate was another New Zealander, Paul Radisich, who more recently carved himself a formidable reputation at the wheel of the works-backed Ford Mondeo in the British Touring Car Championship. The son of a racing father, Radisich was then a keen, thrusting young single-seater charger whose ambitions matched those harboured by Damon.

In the second round of that title chase, Damon posted his first British F3 finish with tenth place on the Silverstone club circuit at the wheel of the MTR Ralt RT30/86. The race was won by fellow

Another step up the ladder. Aiming the Murray Taylor Racing Ralt out on to the Grand Prix circuit at Brands Hatch during the 1986 Cellnet Super Prix.

Brit Andy Wallace, then regarded as a future F1 talent, with a Reynard 863.

The F3 front-runners of the moment were Wallace, Ulsterman Martin Donnelly and another Brazilian, the pint-sized Maurizio Sandro Sala. It was chasing Sala that Damon produced his best result of the year at Snetterton in round 13 of the championship, finishing less than three seconds behind his winning rival after 25 laps of the tricky 1.917-mile Norfolk aerodrome circuit.

Hill's other top six finishes came at Oulton Park (fourth), Donington Park and Zandvoort, Holland (fifth on both occasions) and a sixth place at Brands Hatch. His final position of ninth equal in the points table was shared with Keith Fine and was a single point adrift of David Hunt, kid brother of ex-World Champion James.

He was headed by four other Brits in the ratings; Wallace, who won the title; Donnelly, who finished third behind Sala, Julian Bailey (sixth) and Tim Davies (seventh). On the face of it, Damon had not set the world afire. He had shown flair on many occasions, leading at Oulton Park and Zandvoort, but somehow the late-season races were less kind to him and the anticipated breakthrough never quite came.

He learned a great deal about car control, of course. 'My mechanic Kevin Corin showed me how to learn what I should be learning about and Murray was good at helping me keep up my self-confidence.

'You control a car with three things; the power, the brakes and the steering. In F3 there is no power. The brakes are so good that you only use them 50 yards before a corner and, if you have excessive understeer, you are out of control the way I see it.

'Neutrality [of handling] is the aim. Only if it's wet can you drive round a problem. At the Cellnet Super Prix (in 1986) my front wings dropped backwards so I had front-end lift and massive understeer, but I could chuck the car into corners becuase I knew it was understeering so much it couldn't spin. But in the dry? Forget it!'

For 1987, Damon switched to the Cellnet-Ricoh-backed Intersport Racing outfit. Run by Glenn Waters, who had been Mario Andretti's mechanic at Lotus during the American's World Championship winning season in 1978, Hill would make considerable progress throughout a season in which he eventually found himself partnering Martin Donnelly, who made a mid-season transfer into the line-up.

This was Johnny Herbert's championship year with the Eddie Jordan Team. The Intersport duo piled on the pressure in the closing stages of the season after Donnelly had confirmed Hill's earlier complaints that the TOM's Toyota engines powering the cars were short on power.

Improvements were duly made and the Intersport cars were transformed into the British F3 pacesetters during the second half of the year, the first sign of that performance upsurge coming when Hill led Donnelly home to an impressive 1-2 success at Zandvoort in June.

Damon went on to dominate the race at Donington Park in August before overheating delivered him the agonizing disappointment of being forced to retire in the closing stages. But he more than made up for that with an excellent win in the race held at Spa-Francorchamps, home of the Belgian Grand Prix, in the second week of September.

He finished fifth in the British championship behind Herbert, Bertrand Gachot, Donnelly and Thomas Danielsson.

Herbert, who would suffer terrible leg injuries when he crashed in a

Damon (right) with race winner Maurizio Sandro-Sala and third placed man Paul Radisich after scoring his best F3 result of 1986 with second place at Snetterton on 10 August.

Formula 3000 race at Brands Hatch the following summer, would later bounce back to take his place in Formula 1, first with Benetton, then with Lotus.

On the eve of the 1994 Grand Prix season, he admitted that Damon hadn't been a front-running contender during his own F3 title year. 'My main threat came from Bertrand Gachot,' he reflects. 'Damon wasn't really a threat, but he's stuck to it and driven well. I've come all the way up through the junior formulae with him and the fact remains that he's got the job done and is going to be one of the men to beat in 1994.'

In 1988, Hill remained in the Cellnet-backed Intersport team alongside Donnelly, but while Finnish rising star J. J. Lehto eased his way to the Championship in his Pacific Racing Reynard, Damon sometimes found his most heated opposition coming from his team-mate from Ulster.

On the face of it, Damon did pretty well. He won early in the season at Thruxton and bagged victory in the prestigious British Grand Prix supporting race at Silverstone. But Donnelly frequently out-shone him in the first half of the season, using the team's 1987 specification Ralt RT31 chassis, and while it seemed as though Hill felt a little more comfortable with the latest RT32, once Martin had made a mid-season graduation to Formula 3000, his campaign fell apart towards the end of the year.

Third place in the final championship stakes behind Lehto and Gary Brabham was, in reality, a disappointment after starting the season with high hopes of taking the title for himself.

Donnelly reflects happily on his rivalry with Damon during that sometimes frantic year. He was speaking at the start of 1994, over three years since his own professional career came to an abrupt end following a huge accident during practice for the 1990 Spanish Grand Prix. His Lotus-Lamborghini was destroyed in a horrific accident and he hovered between life and death for several days.

Martin now runs his own team in the minor league Vauxhall Lotus and Vauxhall Lotus Junior British national championships. These days he presides over racing which is every bit as frenetic as those days he spent in F3 with Damon.

'In 1988 we were both invited to take part in a non-championship race at Knockhill, up in Scotland,' he recalls with enthusiasm. 'The event organizers tried to attract a top class field and Damon spent a lot of time doing promotional work for Cellnet in the run-up to the race.

'As things turned out, they didn't get a big field of Class A runners, so Damon and I had it pretty much to ourselves in practice, trading times. One of us was going to win.

'Throughout practice we traded fastest times and I got pole by 0.2 sec. Then when the official times were published, they gave pole to Damon. Well, for me, that was like a red rag to a bull. All the team's timing sheets had me quicker, and I ended up protesting my team-mate. But they weren't about to reverse it.

'Then they told us they were going to have a staggered two-by-two grid, rather than the side-by-side grid that the Formula Ford competitors were going to use, so that was another row! But when we lined up on the grid, they said that it was going to be two-by-two after all, so now Damon was fit to be tied.

'Anyway, come the race, I knew that Damon's pole position meant that he was going to be on the dusty side of the circuit, off-line. We

Celebrating third place behind Johnny Herbert (centre) and Gary Brabham after the second round of the 1987 British F3 Championship, again on the Brands Hatch GP circuit.

Main picture *Big Day. Damon's Ralt leads the similar car of Gary Brabham and J. J. Lehto's Reynard en route to a 1-2-3 finish in the 1988 British Grand Prix supporting F3 classic.*

Inset *At speed with the Cellnet/Ricoh Ralt RT31-Toyota which he used to take fifth place in the 1987 British F3 Championship.*

After his Silverstone GP F3 win Damon (centre) shares the rostrum with Gary Brabham (left) and John Penfold, winner of the 'second division' Class B category in this event.

got off the line together and I held him tight over on his side of the track all the way to the corner. We both locked up our front wheels, but he was still on the dirt and off he went, straight into the tyre barrier!

'I went on to win the race, and the following day when I got home there was a message summoning me to a meeting at the Cellnet headquarters in London the following day. I got there just after Damon and we were both given our P45s. We were fired!

'We had to do a bit of grovelling, I can tell you, over the next couple of weeks to get ourselves reinstated!'

For all this rivalry, Donnelly insists that he continues to get on well with Damon. 'But once we got to the circuit and the helmet visors came down, then we were big competitors,' he grins.

He is full of admiration for his old team-mate's achievements. 'I used to rate him a little bit like Mansell, I suppose,' says Martin. 'Not an abundance of natural talent, he has worked at it. I believe, given the chance in Formula 1, he will get better and better.'

David Tremayne, now Executive Editor of *Motoring News* and the newspaper's F3 correspondent during the mid-1980s, came to know

Damon extremely well as he battled his way up through the junior formulae. He was always impressed with the way Hill handled himself, and is not totally surprised that he's punched his way through to the big time. By the same token, he concedes that he certainly wasn't the most obvious talent.

'From early on it became obvious that he didn't seem to think that the world owed him a living,' says Tremayne. 'In 1986, he was very undramatic, unobtrusive and very smooth. He didn't look all that quick, though, and took time to play himself in.

'He was determined, but I always thought that Perry McCarthy, for example, was the hungriest driver I ever saw at that time. When it came to the 1987 F3 season, Johnny Herbert was head and shoulders above the rest – then came Donnelly, McCarthy and Hill. In 1988 it was Damon, Donnelly again and J. J. Lehto who were the guys to watch.

'Damon always made the most of any opportunity he got. On a personal level, I always found him terrific – good company and with a sense of humour. He's always himself, not like a lot of the guys today in top line racing.

'Talking about his progress in 1993, the difference is now that he's smart enough to know that you've always got to keep working at it, which perhaps Johnny Herbert, for example, has taken longer to realize.

'Damon has done what he's done very carefully, without making any waves. The most important thing was that by the time he got to Formula 1 he was his own man rather than Graham's boy. I wouldn't write off his chances of doing bloody well in 1994, even if he just follows Ayrton home.

'There's not much downside to Damon. He can be a bit moody, but that's because he's so hard on himself. He can be very quiet and reflective when something is pissing him off. But in 1993, for example, I was very impressed with the great dignity he displayed when those wins at Silverstone and Hockenheim went away from him.'

In 1988 he also married Georgie, his long-time girlfriend and supporter. On 3 March 1989 she gave birth to the first of their two sons, Oliver, who was unfortunately a Downs syndrome baby. With a mixture of practicality, fortitude and commitment, they shrugged aside initial suggestions that he should be cared for in a specialist

Main picture *Damon's Ralt RT32-Toyota heading for second place in the Macau F3 Grand Prix of 1988.*

Inset *Damon nips inside Antonio Tamburini's Dallara-Alfa Romeo during the 1988 Monaco F3 supporting race in which he finished sixth, one place ahead of team-mate Martin Donnelly.*

home and decided to bring him up as normally as possible in a caring family environment.

'It was an awful thing for both of us, particularly for Georgie,' says Damon. 'I think in my twenties I very much wanted to force my own plan on my life. I wanted things to happen my way and tended to battle on in one direction, not allowing anything to affect me.

'But after a while you realize that things are either going to happen or they're not. As long as you can say you've done your best, then you should be satisfied.' Their second son, Joshua, was born, fit and well, on 9 January 1991.

After three years in Formula 3, Damon now faced something of a dilemma at the start of the 1989 season. He needed to progress into Formula 3000, the next rung up the ladder towards Formula 1. But acute lack of finance stood in his way.

Formula 3000 is international single-seater motor racing's 'second division'. It supplanted Formula 2 at the end of 1984, catering for single-seaters using ex-Formula 1 3-litre Cosworth engines-equipped with a mandatory electronic rev limiter in order to reduce mechanical wear and tear, thereby – in theory at least – containing costs to a reasonable level.

Damon had no sponsorship available, but was invited to drive in a round of the British F3000 championship – little more than a club racing affair – at Oulton Park early in the season, where he finished third in a year-old Reynard-Cosworth behind Andrew Gilbert-Scott and Gary Brabham. It proved nothing.

Then he accepted an invitation to drive in a Porsche 962 entered by Richard Lloyd Racing in the Le Mans 24-hour sports car classic. Sharing with fellow Brit David Hobbs and Sweden's Steven Andskar, they completed 228 laps – about two-third distance – before being sidelined with engine failure.

A few weeks later, Damon's career was thrown a lifeline from an unexpected source. The Japanese Mooncraft F3000 team had been operating a European Championship programme out of its Reading base for Ukyo Katayama who was also commuting back and forth to Japan to take in rounds of their national championship as well.

Right *On the rostrum at Macau celebrating with winner Enrico Bertaggia (centre) and third placed man Otto Rensing.*

Inset *Taking the next step. Damon getting a taste of Formula 3000 late in 1988 with the GA Motorsport Lola, en route to retirement at Zolder and* **Main picture** *a brighter eighth place at Dijon-Prenois.*

'He really wasn't up to all this travel and, in addition, had major language problems with the engineers,' recalls team manager John Wickham. 'So we arranged a test session at Snetterton for Damon and Perry McCarthy, both of whom lapped at much the same speed. But the sponsors liked the idea of Damon and we signed him for the rest of the season.'

Sadly, the Mugen-engined Mooncraft MC-041 didn't amount to a particularly competitive piece of equipment, but it succeeded in keeping Damon in play.

He ran five races with the car, the best result being a 15th place at Dijon-Prenois, two laps down on the winning Lola driven by Erik Comas. At Enna-Pergusa in Sicily he retired the car with overheating, was out early at Brands Hatch with gear linkage problems and didn't even get to the start of the Birmingham Super Prix street race after the Mooncraft broke a driveshaft on the warming-up lap.

His only other result was 16th on the Le Mans Bugatti circuit where his father had led the 1967 French Grand Prix at the wheel of a Lotus 49. Even so, Damon had impressed people with his single-mindedness.

'He was very good to work with,' continues Wickham. 'Very concise and perceptive in his comments on the car. I think his F3 career had been a bit up and down, but I was impressed. He was certainly getting better and better by the time he drove for us.'

Journalist Tony Dodgins echoed these sentiments in the annual Formula 3000 review that autumn in the prestigious *Autocourse* annual: 'The car appeared large and unwieldy and it was Damon Hill who had the dubious privilege of driving it from Enna onwards. To his great credit, Damon gave it everything he had and qualified everywhere, although he had a fight on his hands come race day.'

For 1990, Damon's prospects took a distinct turn for the better. He was invited to contest the International F3000 championship driving a Lola-Cosworth T90/50 for the Milton Keynes-based Middlebridge Racing outfit, and effort which rewarded him with a best result of second place at Brands Hatch. He started on pole position three times, recorded two fastest laps and led five races.

His new Lola was desperately short of test mileage when he took part in the opening race of the season at Donington Park and he failed to qualify, but the second round at Silverstone yielded a far

Making the best of a bad job. Damon wrestling with the Footwork team's Mooncraft-Mugen MC-041 in the 1989 Formula 3000 round at Dijon-Prenois. He impressed many people with his dogged handling of this difficult-to-drive machine.

Splashing round Brands Hatch with the Middlebridge team's Cosworth-engined Lola T90/50 where Damon would score his best result of the season with a second place to Allan McNish's similar Mugen-powered car.

Above *Hockenheim produced a dreadful weekend for Damon in 1990. He started his Middlebridge Lola from pole position to lead on the opening lap – and then threw it away by spinning off at the right-hander beyond the pits.*

Right *Happy chap. Damon manages a smile for the camera, even though his 1991 Formula 3000 season with the EJR/Barclay squad yielded little in the way of hard results.*

more representative performance.

Test sessions at both Pembrey, in South Wales, and at Monza had significantly improved the car's set-up, and Damon qualified confidently in third place behind the DAMS' team Lolas of Allan McNish and Comas. He made a terrific start to take an immediate lead which he held commandingly for 16 of the 41 laps before an electrical problem caused his retirement out on the circuit.

Lola engineer Duncan MacRobbie admitted that he 'couldn't be more impressed' at Hill's showing: 'He's very level-headed and has given us some *excellent* feedback, and the way he led the race was amazing for someone who hasn't raced for so long.

'He was marking every corner exactly the same on every lap and was totally in control. We've got a lot of time for him and, mark my words, he'll win races.' Well, yes – but not in the Lola, as things transpired!

In the aftermath of the Silverstone race, Damon was understand-

Main picture *Damon's EJR/Barclay Lola T91/50 chases Laurent Aiello's similar car round the infield hairpin at Rome's Vallelunga circuit during the opening round of the 1991 International F3000 series. Aiello crashed, but Damon continued to finish a strong fourth.*

Inset *Hockenheim brought bad luck again for Damon in 1991. This time his EJR/Barclay Lola was out early with a stuck throttle.*

ably angered by certain national newspaper stories which claimed that he'd inadvertently flicked off the ignition switch – rumours made all the more agonizing when the car fired up immediately on its return to the paddock.

'I'm fed-up and very angry,' he said. 'I just don't know where the story came from. It makes me look a complete idiot.'

He was on pole again for the fifth round at Monza, leading the early stages before encountering more technical problems and dropping to 11th. In the seventh round at Hockenheim, in the supporting race to the German Grand Prix, he started from the front yet again, led the opening lap – and then spun off after riding over the bevelled kerb on the right-hander leading out of the stadium beyond the pits.

He bounced back from that disappointment to take second to McNish at Brands Hatch – his best result – and then rounded off the season with two more retirements and a 10th place. The bottom line was a joint 13th place in the final F3000 championship points table, a result which in no way reflected the outstandingly promising form he had displayed throughout the year.

For 1991, Damon drove for Barclay Team EJR which was the Middlebridge team again, but now using sponsorship which had been provided by Eddie Jordan who was busy laying plans for his graduation to Formula 1 the following year and was no longer directly involved in the junior category.

After such a promising 1990 season, Damon's resilience was put under a great deal of pressure as the new Lola T91/50 chassis was no match for the latest rival Reynard 91D. Although he finished seventh in the final points table, this was largely because of a strong third place in the final race at Nogaro where he finished third behind Christian Fittipaldi and Alessandro Zanardi – in a Reynard borrowed from Karl Wendlinger!

However, as we shall see in the next chapter, another key factor had entered Damon Hill's professional racing career which went a long way towards keeping his optimism alive.

He secured himself a testing contract with the Williams-Grand Prix team, the famous Didcot-based equipe which was currently suging back to World Championship-winning form with Nigel Mansell as its number one driver.

Damon racing wheel-to-wheel in FF1600 on the approach to Surtees Bend, Brands Hatch, in the Manadient Racing Van Diemen.

Testing the Ralt RT32 at Snetterton in its Macau GP livery prior to taking second place in the 1988 race through the streets of the former Portuguese colony.

Slithering out of the Thruxton chicane in the Intersport-run Cellnet/Ricoh Ralt-Toyota during a round of the 1988 British F3 Championship.

Practising the Mooncraft F3000 car for the 1989 Birmingham Super Prix – Damon didn't even get to the start as the car failed on the warm-up lap!

With the Middlebridge Racing Lola T90/50 contesting the Enna-Pergusa round of the 1990 International F3000 championship.

Left *Damon with the EJR/Barclay Lola T91/50 at Mugello in 1991 where he retired in a first lap accident.*

Right *Team manager Ray Boulter (in white jacket) directs work on the EJR/Barclay Lola while Damon waits patiently in the cockpit.*

Damon (right) attempts to avoid team-mate Vincent Sospiri who has lost the rear wing of his EJR/Barclay Lola.

End of term photograph for the International F3000 class of '91. Damon is third from the left in the front row, sandwiched between title-winner Christian Fittipaldi (left) and Allan McNish. Sixth from left is Italian girl Giovanna Amati who Damon would succeed in the Brabham F1 team early the following season.

Damon celebrating his last outing in Formula 3000. On the rostrum at Nogaro, 1991, after taking third place behind new champion Christian Fittipaldi (centre) and Alessandro Zanardi.

First time out in the Brabham-Judd BT60B – a revamped version of the car which had previously been powered by a Yamaha V12.

Above *New livery in time for the 1992 French Grand Prix didn't lead to the hoped-for sponsor – and didn't improve the ageing Brabham's form!*

Below *Keeping an eye on the mirror during the 1992 British Grand Prix at Silverstone – Martin Brundle's Benetton, en route to third place, comes up to lap Damon in the Brabham.*

Right *Damon signals the mechanics to fire up the Brabham BT60B in the pit garage at Silverstone.*

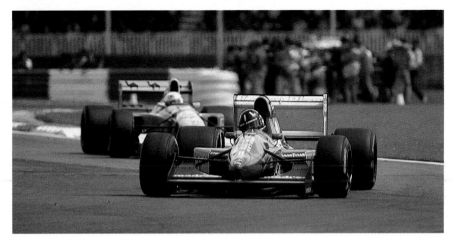

Made it! In company with Frank Williams on the day Damon was confirmed as Prost's team-mate for 1993.

Strapped in and ready to go.

A famous name once more appears on the flanks of a front-line F1 challenger.

Damon gets acquainted with the Williams-Renault FW15C during a mid-winter test at Estoril.

Together with Georgie on holiday prior to the 1993 South African Grand Prix.

Heading for his first helping of World Championship points. Damon in the Williams FW15C on the way to second place behind Senna's McLaren in the 1993 Brazilian Grand Prix at Sao Paulo's Interlagos circuit.

Preparing for the off on the front row of the grid at Donington Park – European Grand Prix, Easter 1993.

Catching up with his reading.

Left and below
Posing with the Renault Safrane saloon – one of his company cars, off track.

Left *Celebrating his second successive second place to Senna. Donington Park, European Grand Prix, 1993.*

That historic day. Damon may have had the track pretty much to himself at Hungaroring during his run to victory in the 1993 Hungarian Grand Prix, but the pressures from within were immense.

Release at last! On the podium after his first Grand Prix win.

Prost leads the opening lap of the 1993 Belgian Grand Prix at Spa-Francorchamps as the pack brake for Les Combes. Damon is in third place, having an anticipatory look up the inside of Senna's McLaren.

Diving inside Aguri Suzuki's Footwork during his memorable climb through the field in the 1993 Portuguese Grand Prix.

• CHAPTER FOUR •

Into F1 by the back door

IN EARLY 1988, Damon Hill had a test in a 1.5-litre Cosworth V6 turbocharged Benetton B187 at the Paul Ricard circuit in southern France. It was an event of limited significance which neither raised his hopes for the future, nor prematurely dashed his prospects.

Contemporary front-line Grand Prix teams run test programmes throughout the year in parallel with their racing commitments, both for the purposes of evaluating new technical development, and as a useful way for team managers to keep an eye on the recent form of the next crop of hopefuls intent on elbowing aside those who have achieved full-time tenure of an F1 cockpit.

. . . getting one's backside into a Grand Prix car on a regular basis is as much a matter of timing and good fortune as having firm credentials

By the end of 1987, Damon was sufficiently prominent a member of the British F3 fraternity to merit such a try-out, and Benetton, which was fast developing something of a reputation for evaluating more than most from amongst the junior brigade, was happy to give him the chance – with no strings attached.

Benetton team manager Peter Collins remembers that Damon was serious-minded, steady and surprisingly fast. 'He went very well, to be honest,' he recalls. 'In fact, he did a rather better job than when we tested Martin Donnelly in the same car at Estoril.'

The problem was that testing opportunities of this kind seldom stand the test of cross-reference with times set by the car's regular drivers. This is particularly so at Paul Ricard, a circuit on which lap times are crucially influenced by wind conditions and ambient temperature. Damon's experience was routine, and of no immediate significance.

He would slog on through the next two and a bit seasons of F3 and F3000 without any talent spotters singling him out as an obvious, overlooked talent. Yet a study of the history book reminds us that getting one's backside into a Grand Prix car on a regular basis is as much a matter of timing and good fortune as having firm credentials delivered by hard results in the junior formulae.

If winning F3 championships had been the only index by which one judged the potential of Britain's rising stars, then Nigel Mansell would never have got his feet off the bottom rung of the ladder.

Back in 1979 the Birmingham driver caught the eye of a perceptive journalist, Peter Windsor, who drew his form to the attention of the Lotus team manager Peter Collins, later the man to give Hill the run in the Benetton.

Colin Chapman's ear was duly bent, Mansell got a Lotus F1 test drive and the vital lock was sprung on his career. It may have taken another six years before Mansell finally found himself in the right place to win Grands Prix as a member of the Williams team, but once presented with the path into full-time F1 he held on to it with a tenacity and resilience which enabled him to weather those interim years of disappointment.

By the end of the 1980s Williams had become one of the most technically accomplished teams on the Grand Prix scene. By 1990, it had also become clear that the pressures of testing in addition to a world-wide racing schedule were becoming too much for team drivers Thierry Boutsen and Riccardo Patrese to manage on their own.

This is in no sense a criticism of the two men, merely a reflection of the sheer volume of work the team needed to get through in order to assess all the technical developments it had in the engineering pipeline. Consequently, Frank Williams and his technical director

A taste of things to come. Damon sampling one of the Williams FW14s during the 1991 season, early in his career as the Williams team's official test driver.

Renewing an old association. Damon attempting vainly to qualify the Brabham-Judd BT60B for the Spanish GP at Barcelona's Circuit de Catalunya. His father Graham scored the last F1 victory of his career driving for the same team – in the 1971 Silverstone International Trophy.

Patrick Head decided to appoint a full-time test driver.

The lucky man was Mark Blundell, then 23 and one of the most promising new names to have been thrown up by the junior single seater league. Throughout 1989 and 1990 Blundell acquitted himself splendidly in this task, helping to develop the semi-automatic transmission system which Nigel Mansell would eventually use to such good effect on his return to the team in 1991, as well as working closely in conjunction with Renault on the development of the powerful 67-degree V10 engine.

Mark never put a wheel wrong nor a mark on one of the team's cars. He impressed Patrick Head with his sensible approach and intelligent feedback. Yet, with no prospect of a full-time Williams drive on the horizon for 1991, he was understandably anxious to go F1 racing on his own account.

. . . he got the Williams test driving deal at a time when there was little else going for him

---

Thus motivated, he signed for the Brabham-Yamaha squad, gained some racing experience and then was thrown back onto the market at the end of that season when the team – by then facing financial problems – failed to renew his contract for the following year.

During 1991, Blundell also continued to do some test driving for Williams but this gradually diminished. Free of his own F1 obligations, Damon was signed to take over this role. Both he and Blundell, who went on to be chief test driver at McLaren in 1992 before rejoining the F1 circus with Ligier in 1993, agree that one could not have put a price on the experience it gave them.

Away from the pressures of learning the F1 business in the pressure-cooker intensity of a Grand Prix weekend, they not only had the opportunity to learn the ropes at the wheel of a Grand Prix car, but rode the crest of the wave of the latest technology. They were not having their first taste of F1 motoring in a tail-end plodder of a car, but in one of the front-running teams of the moment, complete with the engineering back-up most drivers could only dream of.

'I had been driving for the Middlebridge Formula 3000 team and its boss, John MacDonald, was the one I had to thank for putting me in touch with Frank Williams,' recalls Blundell. 'Interestingly, Damon would then follow the same route – a Middlebridge F3000 drive, the Williams test contract and a drive in F1 for Brabham. But Damon then got the big break . . .'

It has to be said that Damon was not universally rated at the time as a condidate for top honours. That said, he got the Williams test driving deal at a time when there was little else going for him, and made the whole project work splendidly in his favour.

Like Mansell's early success in getting his own shoulder to the F1 door, Damon's performance as the official Williams test driver served as a reminder that success in this business doesn't depend on dazzling natural talent alone. Equally crucial is the ability to grab an opportunity with both hands and capitalize on its potential to the absolute maximum.

Perhaps it goes without saying that Blundell has since reflected that, had the cards fallen differently, he might have found himself in the cockpit of the Williams-Renault for 1993. Mark is a realist, scrupulously fair and objective in all his comments, and certainly not one to bear a grudge.

Yet, at the height of the 1993 Grand Prix Season, as he struggled to produce some decent performances with the Ligier JS39 – a car which, ironically, shared the same powerful Renault V10 engine as Damon's Williams – Blundell sometimes seemed rather wistful when he considered his rival's good fortune.

How does Mark rate Damon? In reality, it's not really a question he wants to be asked. After many years with only Mansell and Derek Warwick for the British fans to cheer, in 1992/93 there was suddenly a welcome avalanche of home-grown F1 talent for the nationalistic crowds to support.

Mansell may have chosen to shape his personal professional racing future on the US Indycar scene, but almost from nowhere there were five Brits on the scene to more than fill the vacuum caused by the departure of the 1992 World Champion. In addition to Hill and Blundell, there was Johnny Herbert at Lotus, Martin Brundle at Ligier and Derek Warwick at Footwork. All of them were now free of Mansell's shadow, all competing ferociously for his mantle.

Blundell weighs his words with scrupulous care. 'It's a difficult one that,' he ponders. 'All I would say was that, from Formula Ford

Left *Determination. Damon strapped in the Brabham BT60B cockpit, waiting to give of his best. It was quite a contrast to the Williams-Renault FW14B which he was testing as part of his 'day' job!*

onwards, there were four or five guys who did most of the winning – Johnny Herbert, Bertrand Gachot, me and a couple of others. Damon was only an occasional winner but, as he has since proved, you need the complete package to achieve success.

'I would take nothing away from Damon and his achievements. But I don't think any of us would have any qualms about reflecting on what he achieved before he drove the Williams. We all know the score, Damon included.'

Blundell was not attempting to be enigmatic. He was only giving voice to what most of us thought from the journalistic touchline. During his junior league years Damon Hill was a good runner, tough and competitive. But there didn't seem to be any obvious spark that made one think 'there is a future champion.' But, as he would subsequently remind us, professional racing drivers are learning all the time, improving their technique and gaining from experience. And Damon has learned more than most.

By the start of the 1992 season, the Brabham F1 team was limping along in disarrary, a shadow of its former self. It was 30 years since the first F1 car to carry the team's name had made its debut in the German Grand Prix at Nürburgring in the hands of Sir Jack Brabham.

Sir Jack would go on to win the 1966 World Championship and his team-mate Denny Hulme made it a back-to-back success by retaining the title the following year. Brabham retired from driving at the end of 1970, sold the company to his long-time confederate Ron Tauranac who in turn sold it to Bernie Ecclestone in time for the start of the 1972 season.

Ecclestone, the quick-witted, shrewd and hard-bargaining entrepreneur who has been largely responsible for the transformation of F1 into a world-class sport over the past two decades, ensured that Brabham prospered under his stewardship. From 1974 to 1985 the team was firmly established in the front rank and produced the machinery which carried Nelson Piquet to the first two of his three World Championships in 1981 and 1983.

By 1990, however, the team had been sold to Swiss businessman Joachim Luhti and was fading fast. In 1991 the team – by now controlled by the Middlebridge Group – secured an engine supply partnership with Yamaha which proved promising and moderately successful; team drivers Martin Brundle and Mark Blundell achieving a handful of top six finishers between them with the Japanese company's V12 engine.

However, at the end of that season, Yamaha decided to switch its engine deal to the rival Jordan team and, with the world-wide economic recession biting hard, it was touch and go whether Brabham would make it to the first race of the 1992 season.

Unable to finance the construction of totally new cars, Brabham was forced to re-work its existing BT60 chassis to accommodate leased Judd V10 engines in place of the Yamaha V12s. The team signed Belgian F3000 rising star Eric van de Poele, paired with feisty Italian girl Giovanna Amati, from the start of the year, but after the latter failed to qualify in the South African and Brazilian Grands Prix, she was stood down before the European leg of the season kicked off at Barcelona.

Brabham boss Dennis Nursey was obliged by financial necessity to include Amati in the team's line-up, even though he really wanted Damon from the start. A company called Alolique, which now controlled the assets of the Middlebridge Group, had originally planned to run a F3000 programme for Damon, but that project fell apart because of lack of sponsorship. Consequently, Hill had opened the New Year with his ongoing Williams test contract as his sole source of income.

In truth, Brabham was in such a financial plight that there seemed every possibility that the team would close its doors before even contesting that third round of the championship.

'Most of our creditors are being patient,' team director Dennis Nursey assured *Autosport* magazine mid-way through April. 'One or two got impatient, but we've got that sorted out now. Obviously we need money. If we don't get a sponsor or a buyer, it might be that we don't get to Barcelona.

'I'd like to get away with selling only 40 per cent of the team, but could quite easily get rid of 100 per cent. If I cannot sell 40 per cent, it'll have to be 100 per cent. We're talking to people in South Africa,

Italy and two groups in Japan. There is only a slight possibility of not having to sell any of it.'

It was into this uncertain situation that Damon Hill walked, eyes open, to have his first stab at qualifying for a World Championship Grand Prix. Away from the greasepaint and the roar of the crowd, he was still diligently testing away for Williams, so it would be hard to have imagined a bigger contrast in terms of machinery as he strapped himself into the cockpit of the Brabham BT60B for his first qualifying attempt at Barcelona.

The 1992 Spanish Grand Prix was the second such event to be staged at the new, purpose-built Circuit de Catalunya near Montmelo, about 30 km north of Barcelona. It was 24 years since Graham Hill had won the same race at Madrid's twisty Jarama circuit at the wheel of a Gold Leaf Lotus 49.

All Damon could do was give as good an account of himself as possible before the axe fell

---

That occasion was the first World Championship qualifying round contested by Chapman's famous team after the trauma of Jim Clark's death, and Hill Senior was shouldering the responsibility for rebuilding its shattered morale.

Now Damon faced a more modest psychological challenge, albeit no less daunting from the standpoint of sheer competitive intensity. The Brabham team's position was such that anything he could bring to the party was to have a bearing on its ultimate fate. Brabham was on the slippery slope to oblivion even before he slipped behind the wheel. All Damon could do was give as good an account of himself as possible before the axe fell.

The team was balanced on such a commercial knife-edge that its transporter was impounded at Le Perthus, on the Franco-Spanish border, en route to this race. The police were acting on a court order obtained by a company called Pol Marketing who were claiming £30,000 owing for the provision of Brabham's corporate hospitality at the previous year's French Grand Prix.

For a few hours, it looked like a very sticky situation indeed. But the transporter was permitted to continue after disgorging the spare

Left *Clipping the kerb at Imola with the Brabham BT60B, this time trying to make the cut for the San Marino Grand Prix. Again, no joy!*

BT60B which was to be held hostage against payment of the debt. That left Hill and van de Poele with the added pressure of knowing if they crashed their race cars, there was no back-up chassis into which they could transfer.

Damon's first day of practice was badly compromised by a serious misfire from the Judd V10 engine. This caused him to stall moments after crossing the line delineating the end of the pit lane. Although only yards away from the Brabham pit, Hill's car was now technically on the circuit and the mechanics were unable to move it until the formal go-ahead had been received from race officials.

That little drama lost the team crucial minutes they could ill afford. Overnight he was a provisional 30th, six places away from making the grid. Then it rained on Saturday, nobody improved their times and he failed to make the cut.

A fortnight later, Hill turned up at Imola for the San Marino Grand Prix only to find ominous evidence that the Brabham financial tightrope had become even more precariously suspended. The team was debarred from taking part in Friday morning's free practice session with engineers from John Judd's company, Engine Developments removing the electronic control boxes from the V10 engines to prevent them being fired up.

The lease fees on the engines were overdue and the control boxes were only re-fitted when the necessary financial guarantees were received in England. More time was lost.

As if that wasn't bad enough, Damon's times in Friday qualifying were disallowed when the Brabham was found to be underweight. On Saturday he missed qualifying by 1.2 sec. Some critics thought Hill was doing himself more harm than good by slogging on with this tail-end also-ran, but, as he pointed out at the time, it was the only chance he had got.

A fortnight later, it was time for Damon to try qualifying at Monaco. He'd been there before as an F3 charger, but the media delighted in drawing comparisons with his father's distinguished record of five victories through the streets of the Principality.

In reality, of course, it was unrealistic to compare the struggling

Brabham-Judd with the sturdy BRMs or superbly competitive Lotus 49s which Graham had used to earn himself the soubriquet 'Mr Monaco'. It would have been more realistic to liken the BT60B with the frail Lotus 12 in which Graham had made his Grand Prix debut in the Mediterranean resort some 34 years earlier. On that unmemorable occasion, it retired when it lost a wheel at the chicane.

Damon failed to make the cut by 0.4 sec, so the tabloids were deprived of their story. He retired to his modest hotel at nearby Beaulieu to nurse his wounds. 'When I see Nigel Mansell and Riccardo Patrese passing me out on the circuit, I feel terrible,' he admitted wistfully.

'It's very soul destroying. But I like to think there's a bit of me in that Williams FW14B. I've helped with quite a few of its features . . .'

Ironically, at around the time of the 1992 Monaco race, a rumour surfaced that Damon was under consideration for a drive in the forthcoming Indycar races at Detroit and Portland in the front-running Newman/Haas Lola-Ford team. The plan was for Hill to deputize for the injured Mario Andretti who was nursing badly broken toes following an accident in the Indianapolis 500.

As things transpired, nothing came of the deal. Italian driver Teo Fabi was recruited to drive at Detroit, and Mario struggled back to the cockpit in time for the Portland race. But motor racing fans will have noticed the ironic twist to this story. Within another four months, the Newman/Haas team was destined to play a key role in moving Damon Hill into the F1 limelight when they made a bid for Nigel Mansell.

For the moment, however, the disappointment continued. Engine failures intervened to prevent Damon from qualifying for the Canadian Grand Prix at Montreal, but there was a flicker of commercial hope for the beleaguered team three weeks later when the Brabhams appeared sporting a distinctive new paint job for the French race at Magny-Cours.

Nobody seemed to know much about the 'mystery sponsors', but the revised colour scheme made no difference. On Friday, Damon had gear selection problems in his race car, switching to the spare only to find himself grappling with a misfire. On Saturday, he ended up stranded out on the circuit with an electrical problem, and another Sunday became an enforced day of rest.

Seven days later it was time to tackle the British Grand Prix for the first time. On the face of it, there was nothing about the Brabham-Judd's form to make anybody think either team driver would encounter good fortune on the wide open expanses of Silverstone, but this time the cards just tipped Damon's way.

Admittedly, the weekend began on a disappointing note with Damon's engine failing and van de Poele suffering a water leak. The Belgian's car was repaired, but sensible team strategy decreed that Hill should take it for first qualifying, bearing in mind his intimate knowledge of the circuit. He was also benefiting from better specification Judd V10 engines and some aerodynamic modifications, including a revised undertray, money for which had somehow been squeezed out of the dwindling Brabham budget.

'They were giving me a great big cheer, even though I was almost last'

He managed 26th fastest time and the onset of steady rainfall on Saturday preserved his precious position on the last row of the grid. The race, of course, turned out to be a Nigel Mansell benefit, the Williams team leader totally demolishing his opposition on the way to an unchallenged victory. It was his fifth triumph in a World Championship race on British soil and his army of loyal fans responded by flooding onto the circuit in a manner which made any FA Cup pitch invasion look small beer by comparison.

Almost unnoticed in the crush, Damon completed the race in 16th and last place – four laps down on the winning Williams. He was also treated to a first-hand view of the Mansell-mania on the slowing down lap.

'I was right behind Mansell and thought, "We're not going to get out of here alive," because the place was just awash, just swarming with people.' he told *Autosport's* James Allen. 'I nearly ran over six people. They didn't seem to know that there were other cars on the track, they just saw Nigel and leaped on to the circuit. It was very difficult. They were giving me a great big cheer, even though I was almost last.'

Damon also admitted he was almost in awe of Mansell's perform-

Main picture *Made it at last. The first corner of the 1992 British Grand Prix with Damon's Brabham already dropping away at the back of the field. Ahead of him are Olivier Grouillard (Tyrell), Karl Wendlinger (March), Stefano Modena (Jordan), Pierluigi Martini (Dallara), Gianni Morbidelli (Minardi), and Mauricio Gugelmin (Jordan).*

Inset *On the pit wall at Silverstone, contemplating the efforts of team-mate Eric van de Poele, in company with Brabham team manager John MacDonald.*

ance. 'I must say that I think Nigel deserves it [the adulation] because he's doing a fantastic job and I think that I'd be very pleased to drive that car in a Grand Prix, but I have to say that at the moment I don't think I'm capable of doing the sort of job that he's doing. I don't see how he can lose the World Championship now.'

It was back to more familiar ground at Hockenheim a fortnight later. On that ominous high speed German track through the pine trees near Heidelberg, the circuit which had claimed the life of his father's great team-mate Jim Clark back in 1968, the Brabhams proved hopelessly out-gunned. Again, Damon failed to qualify for the race.

Two weeks further on again, it was time for the Hungarian Grand Prix at Budapest. On the weekend that Nigel Mansell successfully clinched his World Championship crown with a second place finish behind Ayrton Senna's McLaren, Hill's F1 career seemed now to be suspended by a precarious thread.

. . . events had been set in train that would result in Hill hitting the F1 jackpot

---

The Brabham team effort was down to a single car, van de Poele having taken what sponsorship money he had left to the rival Fondmetal outfit. This technically left Brabham in breach of the World Championship regulations, which required it to field a pair of cars in each of the 16 qualifying races.

The team claimed *force majeure* on the basis that Van de Poele had only made his decision to quit on the Wednesday prior to the race, leaving them no time to arrange a replacement driver. As talks to secure Brabham's future went on behind the scenes, Damon went out to qualify.

In the first timed session he was 29th, but the following day, despite crashing one of the BT60Bs, he managed to squeeze in a lap time good enough to earn him 25th place on the 26 car grid. Come Sunday it would be the last time a Brabham F1 car would appear in a World Championship Grand Prix. Damon struggled home 11th, 30 years almost to the week since his father Graham won the German Grand Prix at Nürburgring, the second success of his career.

Brabham failed to make it to the Belgian Grand Prix at Spa a fortnight later. Officially, it was now the end of the road. Damon was back where he had started at the beginning of the year, with only that Williams team test contract to sustain him.

'I suppose that you do occasionally have mixed emotions [about testing],' he reflected to *Autosport*. 'Sometimes I feel that I am so lucky to be able to drive the best F1 machinery in the world, and yet I can't race it.

'In the back of your mind you always think to yourself, "God, I'd love to race this car. I'd love to go to a Grand Prix and race this car," and then you think, "Will that ever happen, or am I just dreaming?"'

Ironically, at the moment the sun was setting on the Brabham team, behind the scenes events had been set in train which would result in Hill hitting the F1 jackpot. Nigel Mansell, riding the crest of a wave of success with the World Championship and a record ten Grand Prix wins under his belt after a splendid 1992 season, was not a happy man.

Having been undisputed number one driver in the team for two years, he now discovered that Frank Williams was about to replace his loyal team-mate Riccardo Patrese with French star Alain Prost. Patrese, one of the most genial and popular members of the F1 fraternity, had spent five years of solid, moderately successful endeavour in the Williams camp. But he was not a true number one and the time had now come for his departure.

Prost, who had spent 1992 taking a sabbatical after being dropped by the Italian Ferrari team before the final race of the previous season, was intent on returning to the F1 maelstrom with his eyes firmly focused on a fourth World Championship. His deal with Williams frankly unsettled Mansell whose own negotiations with the team became protracted, absorbed in peripheral minutiae and, in the end, downright confrontational.

The bottom line was that Mansell, in his Hour of Glory, felt that his position atop the F1 pile would be undermined by Prost's arrival. Having spent 1990 as team-mates in the Ferrari squad, Nigel had reached the conclusion that the Frenchman was a highly political animal, all too adept at turning any situation to his own advantage.

Of course, at the end of the day, Williams was going to have Prost come what may. With about 45 per cent of its overall £25 million

Wrestling the Brabham BT60B round Silverstone, keeping out of the way of the faster cars, kept Damon fully occupied throughout the 1992 British Grand Prix. A year later, he would be at the opposite end of the pack – and people would be keeping an eye out for him!

Rumpled Brabham. Damon wrote off this BT60B during practice for the 1992 Hungarian Grand Prix, but drove the spare car to finish the race and bring down the curtain on 31 years of Brabham F1 team history.

budget being provided by either Elf, the French national oil conglomerate, or Renault (in the form of free engines and technical back-up), there was no way the team was going to bite the hand that fed it so generously.

In the past, Frank Williams had gained something of a reputation as a free spirit, but this time he was unwavering in his commitment to take the politically expedient path. It was not as if he was being asked to recruit an also-ran into his driver line-up, as when Honda had requested he took Japanese driver Satoru Nakajima several years earlier. This was Alain Prost, one of the greatest drivers of the post-war era and a man with a matchless reputation for having a sensitive, intelligent and adept grasp of test and development work.

As Mansell's home run to the title increased its momentum, so the Englishman believed himself to be in a stronger position than ever in the negotiating process. Several times he could have signed a finan-cially advantageous contract for 1993, but he seemed reluctant to commit himself.

Neither Mansell nor Williams would comment on the gossip that this reputed £8 million deal eventually founded on a point of trivia – namely the number of hotel rooms that would be available for Nigel's entourage at each race. But the fact of the matter seems to have been that Williams ran out of patience and eventually offered Mansell a considerably lower figure after Nigel missed the deadline for agreeing the original, much higher offer.

Either way, the details don't matter much now. On the morning of the Italian Grand Prix at Monza, Mansell marched into the media centre and convened a press conference at which he confirmed he was retiring from F1. He had been offered a tempting deal to drive for the Newman/Haas Indycar Lola-Ford team as successor to American star Michael Andretti, himself planning a relocation across the Atlantic in the opposite direction as a member of McLaren's 1993 Grand Prix driver line-up.

Immediately, the F1 rumour mill cranked itself up into top gear. Who would replace Mansell? That same afternoon Martin Brundle sped to his best-ever F1 result with second place at the wheel of his Benetton B193 behind Ayrton Senna's McLaren. The driver from Kings Lynn, who had once driven for Williams at Spa in 1988 when Mansell was unwell, moved into the frame as a possible replacement.

There was also Mika Hakkinen, the highly rated young Finn who had been turning heads with some fine performances in the Lotus-Ford. And there was Damon Hill. On the face of it, Graham's lad looked like an outsider in this particular equation. But he was in the equation. And very firmly.

The next couple of months were, to say the least, nerve-racking for those three candidates. Brundle duly went down to Didcot, talked it through with Frank Williams and a draft contract was agreed. At the last moment, Williams had a change of heart – almost overnight. Nobody knew why – and Frank isn't saying.

Then Keke Rosberg, Hakkinen's manager, went into bat for his young Finnish protégé. On the face of it, Mika looked the favourite. Objectively, he was the one who looked most obviously talented and had the most long-term potential. That Rosberg's links with Williams went back to the early 1980s was another beneficial factor. Keke had driven for Frank through four seasons between 1982 and 1985, winning the World Championship in the first of those years.

Lotus proved the fly in the ointment on this occasion. Claiming, incorrectly, that they had Hakkinen under contract for 1993, they sowed sufficient doubt in Frank's mind for him to abort an agreed deal for Mika to take Mansell's vacant seat alongside Prost.

Rosberg was philosophical about the outcome. 'We had a firm contract,' he recalls, 'but there was no point in forcing the issue. You can't force anybody to go through with a deal they are uncomfortable with.' He brushed aside the disappointment and busied himself with the task of negotiating Hakkinen a testing contract for McLaren.

The 1992 season drifted steadily towards its close.

Ligier's management had a shrewd perception of the value offered by Damon's testing experience

Shortly before nine o'clock on a cool, bright autumn morning I was standing in a queue outside the visa department of the Australian embassy in London's Strand, waiting to get the appropriate stamp in my passport for the long haul to Adelaide for the final race of the year.

A tap on my shoulder alerted me to the arrival of a familiar figure, zipped up against the wind in a black bomber jacket and fingering a portable telephone. Damon Hill was in the queue as well, poised to purchase a £600 bucket shop air ticket to make sure he was in Australia as well.

'I'm going to stand in the back of the Williams garage, just to remind Frank I'm still around,' he grinned. 'And to talk to the Ligier team.'

Make no mistake, Ligier was keen to secure Damon's services. For 1993 they would be entering their second season using Renault's powerful V10 engine. They were having a clean-out of their driving team, dismissing both Belgian Thierry Boutsen and Frenchman Erik Comas. Intent on raising the level of its competitive game, Ligier's management had a shrewd perception of the value offered by Damon's testing experience with Williams and, more to the point, with Renault.

Yet, within the Williams enclave, Damon had powerful and influential supporters. Patrick Head, the team's Technical Director, and his colleague, Chief Designer Adrian Newey, had become increasingly impressed with the way he was developing under their wing.

'In his first year as a test driver, I don't think we were considering him as a potential race driver,' Head told *Autosport* magazine. 'But from about the middle of 1992 onwards he started putting in performances which were looking very impressive.

'He certainly became faster and I'm sure he developed while he was with us. Within the first year he regarded himself as purely a test driver. But I think by the middle of 1992, not only was he desperately trying to qualify the Brabham, but he wasn't thinking of himself being a test driver for 1993.

'So I think it was a mental thing. Maybe his ideal was to drive for us, but he also wanted to show that he was good enough to have a drive with somebody else. So I think he started pushing himself a lot harder.'

Early in December 1992, all that commitment paid off for Damon Hill. He was summoned to Frank Williams's presence and duly drove down the M4 to Didcot from his family home in Wandsworth, south London. His heart was pounding with nervous anticipation as he climbed the stairs at Williams Grand Prix Engineering factory.

There, in Frank's spacious, airy office, Damon Hill's dream came true. With a twinkle in his eye, Williams told him that he'd got the drive. With it went a retainer in the order of £300,000 for a one-year deal. The team naturally retained an option for a further season beyond that.

The money, of course, hardly came into it. Damon would probably have driven for nothing. At 32 years old, he was a veteran by the established standards of F1 newcomers. He had only two Grands Prix under his belt yet was now being welcomed into the motor racing equivalent of Aladdin's Cave.

• CHAPTER FIVE •

Life in the front line

FOR WILLIAMS, THE 1993 Grand Prix season started on an unusual note with two new drivers going into the first race. Generally speaking, Grand Prix teams don't like to change both their key employees at the same time. An element of continuity, not only from the standpoint of technical development but also personal chemistry, is regarded as beneficial.

However, Hill's presence alongside Prost represented that crucial thread of continuity. He hadn't raced for the team before, but his testing experience meant that he knew the ropes. Damon was well acquainted with the Williams environment and familiar with the personnel.

Unquestionably, Hill was popular amongst the mechanics and engineers who found his unobtrusive, low-key approach something of a refreshing counterpoint to Mansell's character which, although dynamically competitive, could also be nerve-jangling in its volatility.

Hill was also well-acquainted with the revised specification of the 1993 Williams-Renault FW15C which the team would use in its latest assault on the championship. The previous summer the sport's governing body had decided – for an avalanche of reasons which need not bother us here – that tyre sizes were to be reduced for 1993.

This meant quite a major revamp to the specification of the Williams-Renault package, and Damon was in at the ground floor when these changes were announced, testing the revised car long before he was confirmed as a full-time team member.

For those fans anxious to hail Damon as Nigel Mansell's logical successor, the opening weeks of 1993 were as manna from the heavens. In a succession of crucial pre-season tests, Damon emerged as quick as, if not quicker, than Alain Prost.

It was all heartening stuff. Perhaps, after all, the English novice was going to give his new French colleague a good going-over. Perhaps Prost had lost his touch during his sabbatical year in 1992. Then perhaps not. Either way, there was an intoxicating element of unpredictability surrounding the run-up to the first race of the season, the South African Grand Prix, scheduled to take place at Johannesburg's Kyalami circuit on 14 March.

. . . still coming to grips with the challenges involved in competing in such exalted company

---

For Damon, this was a baptism of fire. No longer was he driving the old Brabham-Judd, keeping one eye firmly trained on his mirror to avoid holding up the faster cars. Now he was one of the pace-setters, one of the Top Dogs for whom the smaller fry had to watch out. Yet, despite being armed with one of the best cars on the circuit, he was still coming to grips with the challenges involved in competing in such exalted company.

At the end of qualifying he was fourth. Pole position had submitted to the silken precision of Alain Prost, with a lap in 1 min. 15.699 secs. Ayrton Senna, in the highly promising new McLaren-Ford MP4/8, was second on 1 min. 15.784 secs. while Michael Schumacher's similarly powered Benetton crouched alongside and slightly ahead of Hill's Williams on the inside of the second row, three-tenths of a second faster than the Londoner.

Damon had experienced a few troubles on the first day of qualifying. 'A warning light in the cockpit kept coming on intermmitently,' he explained, 'and that forced me to stop in the pits quite a few times. But I managed to get a few laps behind Senna which was very worth-

Can this be happening to me? Damon ponders his new career as Alain Prost's team-mate in the Williams line-up for 1993 at a press conference at the team's Didcot factory just before Christmas 1992.

while because it taught me a few good lines through some of the corners.'

One of the new rules imposed for the Kyalami race included shortening the practice sessions and limiting the number of tyres available to each competing car to seven sets per race weekend. Inevitably that imposed additional pressure on F1's latest crop of newcomers but Damon, for his part, came through the test in characteristically assured fashion. Nevertheless, he was disappointed that he did not improve his time on the second day.

His lack of front-line experience caused him to get tangled up amongst a knot of slower cars during that crucial second qualifying session. By the time he'd found himself a piece of clear track, his last set of practice tyres were five laps old and losing the fine edge of their grip – usually at its optimum two or three laps into a qualifying run. He rounded off the session by spinning after moving off the racing line as he attempted to overtake one of the unwieldy new Lola-Ferraris.

Despite this, fourth place on the grid on his debut for Williams was an excellent effort by Hill. His time had only been bettered by the two established superstars of the previous decade and the man regarded as the most promising new blood. Damon's task was now to insert his previously unremarkable reputation into that latter category.

When it came to the race, Damon blotted his copybook within 10 seconds of the green starting light. Senna made a perfect start while Prost got bogged down slightly, and Hill found himself in second place as the pack slammed into the first, fast bend.

The occasion proved all a bit much for the Englishman. Here he was, in his third Grand Prix, with only the legendary Senna and his McLaren between him and the lead. Anxious to cover himself in glory, he allowed his Williams to get too close to the rear wing of the McLaren as they exited the second part of the corner.

One of the deterrents to close racing in Formula 1 is the aerodynamic turbulence caused by a speeding Grand Prix car. Its profile punches a pretty considerable 'hole' in the air, and the airflow coming off its rear wing at speed makes life quite lively for anybody following closely behind.

In simple terms, if an F1 driver gets too close to the car in front,

The Boss is watching. Frank Williams listens intently as Damon answers the barrage of press inquiries on the day his deal for promotion to F1's front line was announced.

Down to the serious business. Now officially carrying the number zero in acknowledgement of the fact that number one would be left vacant as the reigning World Champion – Mansell – would not be racing in 1993, Damon settles down to preseason testing at Estoril.

109

Right *The white gloves signify that Damon is deputizing for Sonic the Hedgehog at the launch of the Williams team's Sega co-sponsorship deal at Kyalami, 1993.*

he'll find that there is not enough air flowing over the nose wings of his own machine. That crucial airflow produces the downforce which helps stick the front end of the car firmly to the track. Remove it and the front end goes light. Suddenly and frighteningly.

The outcome of all this was that Damon lost control of his Williams and spun wildly in front of the other 24 competing cars. Prost locked up and dodged through on the left, but the Frenchman's success in avoiding smart contact with his team-mate was as much to do with the lucky fact that Damon spun away from the racing line as to any great judgement on his part.

As Prost chased off after Senna, eventually to cement his new Williams relationship by defeating the Brazilian to score a win on his maiden outing, Hill settled down to compose himself in 11th place. Before he had a chance to get his second wind, Damon found himself bundled off the circuit after Lotus new boy Alessandro Zanardi attempted an over-ambitious passing manoeuvre which didn't come off.

Later Damon reflected on his race: 'I made a great start, but I was right up to Ayrton's wing and it was really too much. It caught me out a little. The spin was a mistake; my fault, I put it down to experience.

'I managed to recover and keep going, but it was very difficult to overtake out there. If I had not spun on that lap, I would not have been where I was [down the field] and would not have got into any other trouble.

'I felt Zanardi was taking a big risk by lunging there at the same point on each lap. But I have to take the responsibility. I could not avoid him because Alliot [the French driver Philippe Alliot, driving a Larrousse-Lamborghini] was in my way.'

A fortnight later, the second round of the championship took place in an environment so far removed from Kyalami that it is difficult to believe it was on the same planet. The Formula 1 fraternity swapped the parched, rolling backcloth of the Veldt for the grimy, urban squalor of Brazil's industrial second city, Sao Paulo.

If anybody needs convincing that Brazil is not all surf, sand and willowy blondes, then Sao Paulo must have been put on earth to

achieve that very purpose. Yet the Autodromo Carlos Pace at Interlagos, so named after the popular Brazilian who won his home Grand Prix here in 1975 only to be killed in a light aircraft accident two years later, used to be one of the epic tracks on the international trail.

Originally, Interlagos was a daunting five-mile blind incorporating some of the most challenging high speed corners to be found on any circuit in the world. However, between 1981 and 1989, the Brazilian Grand Prix was staged at Rio de Janeiro's bland Autodromo Riocentro, and by the time it was switched back to Sao Paulo in 1990, Interlagos had been emasculated by a re-design to comform to the latest safety standards.

Yet the passionate enthusiasm of the sophisticated Sao Paulo crowd – weaned on home-brewed heroes such as Senna and the Fittipaldi clan, not to mention 'foreigners' like the Rio-born Nelson Piquet – makes for quite an occasion and there are sections of the circuit which still retain their original appeal.

Damon had to be dissuaded from launching a final challenge to Prost's pole position

In the fortnight separating the first two races of 1993, the sport's governing body FISA made some minor adjustments to the F1 regulations. After experimenting with reduced length practice sessions at Kyalami, the programme now reverted to its 1992 format, with 90 minutes allocated for free practice on Friday and Saturday mornings and an hour of official timed qualifying on both those afternoons.

Now the limitation on running time was confined to a total of 23 laps per car during each morning session and 12 in the afternoon. Anybody doing more than 23 laps in the morning would have the excess docked from their allowance in the afternoon – and anybody completing more than an accumulated total of 35 laps over the two sessions would have any such surplus disallowed.

Quite naturally, Senna was hell-bent on winning this race in his own personal backyard, but the estimated 60 bhp surplus enjoyed by the two Williams-Renault drivers ensured he was kept back in third place by the time the final grid order was published.

Damon felt he did a much better job than he had managed at Kyalami 'although it's difficult to explore the limits of the car on a track like this where I have no previous experience.' Prost's familiarity with Interlagos was emphasized by the fact that he lapped a full second faster than Hill to earn pole position, but Damon was content with the inner belief that he could have gone quicker. Anyway, he had a comfortable cushion of 0.8 sec. over Senna's third placed McLaren.

In fact, Damon had to be dissuaded from launching a final challenge to Prost's pole position. 'It looks good out there,' he said optimistically to Frank Williams over his radio link as he sat strapped in the cockpit, suffused with enthusiasm, as the last few moments of the second qualifying session ticked away.

'No, Damon,' said Williams with a slight sense of amusement. There was a pause. 'It looks *really* good out there, Frank!' repeated Damon. 'No, Damon,' replied his boss. 'I don't want you having the added pressure of having to start from pole position.' And there the matter was left to rest.

Scattered showers were forecast for the race day at Interlagos, but Prost signalled that he was unlikely to be troubled by a wet track when he set a best time 1.2 sec. faster than Hill in the half-hour race morning warm-up session, which so often provides a telling pointer to impending race form.

Sure enough, Prost accelerated neatly away into the lead at the start with Senna cutting through to take an immediate second place ahead of Hill. By the end of the opening 2.687-mile lap, Alain was 1.4 sec. ahead of Senna, with Damon sensibly playing himself in in third place.

Not until lap 11 did Hill feel sufficiently familiar with the race conditions to harness every ounce of his William's performance to haul up alongside Ayrton going into the chicane beyond the pits, slipping neatly inside the Brazilian to take second place.

Observers noted that Senna in no way made life difficult for the English novice as he challenged for his position. 'I got the strong impression that he was sizing me up, seeing what I was like,' said Damon thoughtfully after the race.

Now the Williams duo appeared firmly entrenched in first and second places, but this domination was only destined to last for a

113

Main picture *A quick spin in practice for the 1993 South African Grand Prix.*

Inset *Georgie Hill offers a message of optimism – Kyalami, 1993.*

handful of laps before a heavy shower brushed a corner of the circuit, sending most competitors scampering into the pits to change from slicks to deep-grooved rain tyres.

At the end of lap 28 Damon came in for an 8.05 sec tyre change, but Prost, who was due in next time round, momentarily became confused by a garbled message over the radio link just as he was lining up to enter the pit lane.

The Frenchman had a fraction of a second to make a decision and chose to stay out for another lap. He suspected that, perhaps Damon had been delayed with his tyre change and that he might find the Williams pit preoccupied in servicing his rival. Anyway, another lap would hardly make any difference.

In fact, it proved disastrous. The rain was coming down in stair-rods now at the first corner. Christian Fittipaldi had spun his Minardi, which now stood stationary in the middle of the track, right on Prost's planned trajectory.

In only the fourth Grand Prix of his life, Damon Hill was now in the lead

Alain's Williams hit the puddles, immediately aquaplaning into a gentle spin. It clipped the Minardi and slid straight into the gravel trap on the outside of the corner. Prost was out.

Hill was now in the lead, but with cars spinning in all directions, the organizers deployed the newly-introduced 'safety car'. Having taken a leaf out of the US Indycar book and to eliminate the need to stop a race in the event of a succession of accidents, the F1 cars would now file round at reduced pace behind a high-performance road car driven by a suitably accomplished driver.

These laps so conducted would still count as part of the race distance. Once the debris was cleared up, the safety car would be recalled into the pit lane. The green flag would be waved to indicate 'All Clear' and the serious business of racing would resume.

So now Damon took up position at the head of the queue behind the safety car. The track was cleared and, after seven laps at reduced pace, the green flag was waved and the serious racing got underway again with 37 of the scheduled 71 laps completed.

In only the fourth Grand Prix of his life, Damon Hill was now in the lead. Not just ahead of the pack, moreover, but running in front of Ayrton Senna, probably the most formidable competitor of his generation. Few F1 newcomers have been submitted to such dramatic pressure at so early a stage in their career.

For five laps Damon stormed round at the head of the field. Then, at the end of lap 41, he dived into the pits for a change back onto slicks as the track was now drying out. Ayrton had pursued the same tactics a lap earlier, but Hill just squeezed his Williams back onto the circuit ahead of the Brazilian.

Mid-way round that 42nd lap, Senna saw his opportunity. Going into a slow right-hand turn, he sliced decisively through on the inside. But it was close enough even for Damon to believe that Ayrton had misjudged it. He hadn't.

Now it was Hill's turn to counter-attack. On lap 42 he was 2.2 sec. adrift, but reduced that to 1.5 sec. and 0.9 sec. on his next two circuits of Interlagos. The McLaren's advantage hovered between 0.5 sec. and 1.7 sec for the next few laps, but Damon got into a big slide at the bottom of the hill beyond the pits on lap 50, losing 1.6 sec at a stroke.

Even that set-back didn't break his spirit. On lap 53 Damon produced his own personal fastest lap of the race, closing to within a second of Senna once again. But then he called it a day and eased back to conserve the precious six championship points that went with second place.

'It was a fantastic race,' enthused Hill after descending from the rostrum. 'I could see there was a chance to win, but I couldn't keep up with Ayrton in the closing stages and I was anxious to keep my second place and at last break my Formula 1 duck.

'I realized it was difficult in traffic and Ayrton came past me again following our pit stops to change back onto dry weather tyres. But I had two things to consider. Firstly the fact that I had not finished my first race for the team and, secondly, that Alain was no longer running and it was important that I got my car home to the finish.

'I then lost a small degree of grip from the front tyres and eased back. Caution was my watchword in the closing stages.'

With two of the season's 16 races completed, Damon's second place at Interlagos had secured him joint third place on six points with

Preparing for the off; Damon slides into the cockpit of the Williams FW15C.

On the starting grid at Interlagos prior to the 1993 Brazilian Grand Prix – Williams PR Ann Bradshaw keeps the sun off his brow.

compatriot Mark Blundell in the drivers' championship points table. Senna led the reckoning with 16 points, Prost was second on 10.

For the European Grand Prix at Donington Park on 11 April, Damon Hill's portrait graced the cover of the official programme. The race marked the return of world class international single-seater racing to the famous parkland circuit near Derby for the first time since the epic days of 1937 and 1938 when the legendary German works teams from Auto Union and Mercedes-Benz turned out to do battle in front of capacity crowds.

It was Easter weekend so, of course, the English climate produced characteristically unpredictable conditions. It poured with rain on Friday, was pleasantly sunny on Saturday – allowing the Williams duo to button up the front row of the grid – then bucketed down again on race day, sluicing away the team's chances.

Damon did well to set second fastest qualifying time behind Senna, but Prost was quickest in the dry conditions on Saturday. Damon improved his time and hung on to second place, despite suffering a slight problem with a soft brake pedal which guaranteed him a nerve-racking high speed ride through the plunging downhill Craner Curve section, if nothing else!

It was raining heavily at the start of the 76 lap race and Senna was at his absolute brilliant best, slicing through from fifth place on the grid to out-brake Prost for the lead before the end of the opening lap.

Effectively, Senna had the race won by the end of the fourth lap by which he had an advantage of 7.03 sec. over the Frenchman's Williams. Hill was third ahead of Rubens Barrichello's Jordan-Hart, Jean Alesi's Ferrari and Michael Schumacher's Benetton.

To be fair, Prost refused to let go in the opening stages. As the track surface began to dry, he successfully trimmed back Ayrton's advantage to 3.4 sec. He switched to slicks on lap 19, one lap later than the Brazilian, but then dropped way back with a premature change back to wet weather rubber only three laps later.

This was the first chapter of a dreadfully disappointing race for both Williams drivers. They were both handicapped by some poorly judged rear wing adjustments at their first tyre stops, and were beset by trouble matching the engine revs correctly when the semi-automatic gearboxes were required to change down for the corners.

At the end of the day Hill came home second with Prost a distant third, lapped by Senna's winning McLaren.

Hill succinctly summed up the prevailing conditions. 'It was like a nightmare,' he admitted, 'the worst conditions you would ever want to race in. I don't know how I came second. I felt as if I did not know what was going to happen next for most of the time. The conditions were changing all the time and it was very difficult to predict what tyres to use. It might have been possible to do the whole race on slicks, but it alternated so much that it was difficult to make decisions.'

In fact, Damon had salvaged the best result possible for the team, but Frank Williams made no bones about his disappointment over Prost's performance.

'It is obvious that Alain made a very clever tactical [first] change onto dry tyres, but threw it away with a vastly premature change back to wets, and that was the end of the race,' he said in what, in retrospect, would come to be regarded as an excessively outspoken critique of his number one driver.

'It surprised me that a driver of Alain's experience should make those mistakes, but he doesn't like the wet and he is cautious.' Williams added: 'All tyre choices were initiated and motivated by the driver. Any suggestion that anybody else made these decisions is untrue.'

A clairvoyant would not have been required to deduce that Prost was distinctly unamused by the implications of his employer's remarks. He would later reveal that on the day following the Donington Park race his thoughts first seriously turned towards the possibility of retirement.

It was therefore unfortunate that both Williams and Renault chose to pour petrol onto the flames by producing an absurdly self-conscious, back-tracking communiqué the following day stating, amongst other things, 'that the solidarity uniting Williams, Renault and its drivers, Alain Prost and Damon Hill, is as real in defeat as it is in victory and responsibilities for the actions of the team are shared, not individually apportioned.'

In reality, of course, none of this simmering tension was of any direct concern to Damon. He'd done an excellent job at Donington Park and now concentrated on the fourth round of the Championship, the San Marino Grand Prix at Imola's Autodromo Enzo e Dino Ferrari.

On the face of it, Prost could have expected an easy run to the 24th pole position of his F1 career, but the Frenchman fell victim to problems on Friday, so Damon ended the first day's qualifying fastest by 0.2 sec. after an excellent showing.

Grand Prix qualifying is all about maximizing every moment of track time available, even in the 90-minute untimed sessions which do not count towards grid positions. Prost's efforts in this respect were thwarted when he was pushed off the circuit at the Acque Minerali chicane by an over-eager Jean Alesi in the Ferrari. The two cars remained stranded out on the circuit for the entire balance of the session, depriving both drivers of time in which to make crucial adjustments to their chassis settings in preparation for the afternoon.

'It's very nice to see my name at the top of the time sheets, as taking provisional pole position is a milestone for me,' said Hill calmly on Friday afternoon. 'I've been feeling more confident overall since finishing second at Donington a fortnight ago, and felt that Imola would be good for both me and the car.'

Damon was commandingly quickest again on Saturday morning, this time 0.3 sec faster than Prost. Now he was positively effusive about the performance of his Williams-Renault FW15C.

'I can't believe how easy the car feels to drive in these conditions,' he said openly. 'You concentrate on being nice and tidy, trimming away all the excess drama, and the lap times just flow out so easily. I can't quite take in how good it all felt!'

In the second qualifying session Damon came tantalizingly close to hanging on to provisional pole position. Only catching the Jordans of Rubens Barrichello and Thierry Boutsen, on consecutive laps through the twisty section of the circuit just before the start/finish line, thwarted his ambitions.

As it was, Prost took pole by less than one tenth of a second, but a heavy shower just before the start on Sunday afternoon threw finely-judged predictions out of the window, suggesting that the outcome of this race might be less predictable than expected.

On the slippery track surface, and with all the field starting on deep-grooved rain tyres, Hill got the jump on Prost at the start to accelerate round the long Tamburello left-hander clearly in the lead. Ayrton Senna came muscling through to take an immediate second place, and he hauled up onto Damon's tail as they went down the long straight which leads through a fast right-hander into the braking area for the tricky uphill left-hand hairpin called Tosa.

Having easily out-fumbled Prost in the opening stages of the race, Senna could have been forgiven for thinking that Hill would be a pushover as they went on the brakes for Tosa. Ayrton aimed his red and white McLaren firmly down the inside, intent on slicing through into the lead, but was slightly nonplussed when Damon slammed the door in his face, aggressively positioning his Williams on the left of the circuit to prevent the Brazilian coming through.

At the end of that opening lap Hill came splashing through, a confident 1.8 sec ahead of Senna who had Prost still bottled up behind him in third place. Ayrton now proceeded to pull every heart-stopping trick in the book to keep Prost behind, a strategy which

Charting the opposition. Studying the timing screens during qualifying with Williams Chief Designer Adrian Newey (centre) and FW.

played right into Damon's hands. The leading Williams was 8.6 sec clear of the pack by the time Alain finally prised Senna out of second place on lap seven and set off after his team-mate.

Now the San Marino Grand Prix started to assume a major tactical challenge as the track surface began drying out. As soon as he had been overtaken by Prost, Senna made a lightning quick 5.75 sec. stop to change onto slicks, and Alain followed suit a lap later. Damon waited out until lap 11, stopped to change tyres and just managed to squeeze back into the fray with his lead intact.

Senna and Prost had Hill firmly in their sights as they swooped into Tosa next time round in nose-to-tail formation.

'I just managed to hold off Ayrton as I came out of the pits,' recalled Damon later, 'but I slid slightly wide on a damp patch coming out of Tosa just as he seemed poised to come past. Suddenly, Alain seemed to come from nowhere and overtook us both. Then, when I got to the top of the hill, Senna got inside me, boxed me out going into the next double left-hander, and I found myself back in third place.'

On lap 20, Damon lost 2.5 sec. to the leading pair when Barrichello spun his Jordan across his bows. Next time round, after getting slightly off-line lapping Alessandro Zanardi's Lotus, he slid into the sand trap at Tosa and was out of the race.

'I had been grappling with a slightly long brake pedal movement,' he mused reflectively. 'Then, suddenly, the problem seemed to get worse and I slid off the circuit. I am extremely browned off . . .'

Later, Damon would find himself summoned to Senna's presence and given a wigging for having the temerity to get in his way. 'I told him that I was driving the way I had learned from watching him,' he said innocently. 'I don't think there was much he could say about that.'

The next race was at Barcelona's Circuit de Catalunya, the first track on the 1993 schedule at which Damon had prior F1 experience with the old Brabham BT60B. The Williams-Renaults were running with electronic 'fly-by-wire' throttle mechanisms for the first time, a development which it was hoped, would rid them of the gearbox downchange problem which had so hampered their progress at Donington Park.

Hill finished the first day qualifying in disappointed mood, having managed only third fastest behind Prost and Senna. But on Sunday he battled grimly with Prost for pole position, the two Williams drivers trading fastest laps for much of the hour-long session.

Damon went out on the dot of one o'clock, right at the start of the session. He set the target time with a lap in 1 min. 18.361 sec. – the fastest up to that point.

At eight minutes past one Prost went out to set a 1 min. 20.583 sec. lap, slipped slightly to record 1 min. 20.946 sec. second time round and then did 1 min. 18.683 sec. – good enough for second place.

Thirty-three minutes into the session, Hill embarked on his second run, rocking the opposition by trimming his time to 1 min. 18.346 sec. Seven minutes later, Prost responded with 1 min. 17.809 sec. Pole position! The Old Fox had shown his true mettle, much to the admiration of Patrick Head and the other Williams team engineers. It was a stunning lap.

Cruelly, Hill's run was dashed when his Renault engine expired spectacularly with a piston failure

---

Hill was also quick with praise for his team-mate. 'I must say that I thought I'd done enough for pole position this time,' he said, 'but you can never underestimate Alain!

'I was quite aggressive on my first run, so perhaps I at least managed to make him reach out for it a little more than I have done previously. The danger is, of course, that when you go out too soon, you put your time up for others to shoot at!'

At the start, Hill repeated his Imola performance by getting the jump on Prost when the Frenchman suffered a momentary glitch with his car's semi-automatic gearchange, which forced him to fumble for the manual override. In addition, an apparent wiring fault in the control mechanism of the starting lights caused them to change from red to flashing orange, rather than the intended green.

Despite being not quite certain whether or not the race had really started, Damon managed to get to the first corner a whisker ahead of his team-mate while Senna got equally close to snatching second place as they jostled for position under braking.

Main picture *Braking hard for the tricky Tosa right-hander at Imola during his spell in the lead of the 1993 San Marino Grand Prix. It was this corner which would catch Damon out later in the race.*

Inset *Storming to second place behind Ayrton Senna's McLaren MP4/8 – and ahead of team-mate Alain Prost – during one of many rain-soaked spells in the 1993 European Grand Prix.*

At the end of the opening lap it was a repeat of Imola, with Hill 0.8 sec. ahead, but this time Prost was in second place ahead of Senna. The Frenchman duly settled into his stride, chipping away at Damon's advantage to the point where he could slipstream cleanly past into the lead as the two Williams raced down the straight beyond the pits to start their 11th lap.

By lap 21 Prost had eased out a 2.6 sec. advantage, but this evaporated when he got held up lapping Derek Warwick's Footwork, the Englishman being in equally determined pursuit of Mark Blundell's Ligier in a private battle for 15th place, and understandably unwilling to make way for Prost if it was going to lose him valuable time.

Now Hill was right back on Alain's tail. Indeed, he was very seriously looking for a way past. For the next 20 laps the Williams twosome were scarcely separated by more than a couple of lengths all round the circuit. Cruelly, Hill's run was dashed when his Renault engine expired spectacularly with a piston failure. Only 25 of the scheduled 65 laps were left to run.

Damon believed he could have won. There was no false modesty here, and rightly so on this occasion.

'A very disappointing end to the day,' he shrugged. 'I was well in control of the situation, staying with Alain and watching every move he made and at the same time looking for opportunities without obviously taking a big risk. If there was a good clean pass, I would have taken it.

'I had an excellent start, but a few laps on Alain took the lead. He got a good tow off me and I thought, rather than fight at the corner, it was best to let him go and see what he was going to do. Alain has had a lot more experience in Grand Prix racing than I have, so it was helpful to observe his race tactics. But suddenly the engine just went and that was it. All over!'

As it was, Alain reeled off the remaining laps to post the 47th win of his career. He made the point that there had been no team orders and, on this occasion, his younger team-mate had genuinely presented him with a major headache.

'I think if he had been able to keep going at that pace, I would have been in trouble for sure,' said Prost frankly. 'The race was tiring and maybe one of my most difficult races physically. I don't usually have any problems, but I did today.

'The car was very good at the beginning of the race, but later it started to jump sideways in the corners. Damon was very close to me, and at one stage he was almost on my gearbox, but after he retired I did not need to push so hard.'

For Damon, however, the bottom line was his second retirement in as many races. Moreover, Michael Schumacher's Benetton had stormed home third at Barcelona, earning four valuable championship points which took him past Hill to take third place in the drivers' points table. Now it was off to Monaco for Damon's first serious assault on the circuit which had been the making of his father's glittering reputation.

'Monaco is important to me not simply because my father won here, but because it's one of the world's most famous race tracks, along with Indianapolis and Le Mans,' said Damon during his frustrating 1992 weekend vainly wrestling the Brabham-Judd through the streets of the Principality. He left it unsaid that his father won both those classic races as well.

Twelve months later, in the run-up to his Williams debut at

In conversation with Louis Schweitzer, President and CEO of Renault – suppliers of the powerful V10 engines and a healthy chunk of the Williams team's operating budget.

Monaco, he could be found discreetly, firmly making the point that he wanted to be judged on his own merits, not just as his father's son:

'My father's achievements at Monaco really don't have any bearing on what I do. There is no added incentive for me. It would be lovely to win any Grand Prix.

'Monaco is always a difficult proposition. Its restrictions, the fact that it is a street circuit and its lack of grip all conspire to put you on edge. It's a moving target because, as the weekend goes on, the track gets quicker – so everything you do is a bit of a compromise.

. . . *he wanted to be judged on his own merits, not just as his father's son*

'Trying to qualify the Brabham last year was bloody hard work because I spun off in Casino Square and ended up running all over Monaco trying to get back to the pits to take over the spare car.'

Shrewdly, he played down his prospects for the 1993 race, understandably trying to damp down media speculation that he might follow his father into the winner's circle:

'It will be more nerve-racking for me in the Williams because qualifying will be so vitally important to the outcome of the race, as overtaking there is so difficult.

'I am not sure that the FW15C is as well suited to Monaco as at some other circuits. I think maybe it is not so agile on a street circuit.'

None of this should be interpreted as Hill making excuses in advance. He was just reminding all the over-enthusiastic observers that he was facing bloody reality.

Monaco may be one of the most senseless circuits on the World Championship calendar, a potentially lethal follow-my-leader sop to the champagne-swigging high rollers, an anachronism in an era where circuit safety is one of the cornerstones on which Formula 1 so firmly rests. But, by the same token, keeping away from its unforgiving guard rails calls for a special blend of speed and restraint.

As it transpired, Damon handled things magnificently in the first qualifying session on a track surface which, although brushed by heavy rain, began to dry out appreciably towards the end of that hour-long stint. Controlling frazzled nerve ends to delay one's second run as late as possible may have looked like a high-risk strategy, but it was certainly the way to go.

Damon timed things perfectly. Although Prost was quickest for much of the session, he beat the Frenchman into second place by the decisive margin of 0.6 sec.

'It was just a question of being out there at the right moment,' he shrugged. 'The track was drying quickly – particularly up the hill to Casino Square where the cars are running hard on full throttle – and I managed to time things perfectly.

'It was always going to be a tricky one after that heavy downpour at the start of the session. My plan was to do a time in the first part of the session using the minimum number of laps. I managed that, but then Alain went quicker. In the end, it just came down to the timing of that second run.'

By contrast, things were not destined to go as smoothly in the second free practice session. Coming out of the tunnel onto the waterfront, touching around 170 mph, Damon's Williams suddenly snapped into a violent spin. In clouds of tyre smoke, it pirouetted up the escape road and shuddered to a halt. Amazingly, it didn't touch the barriers!

It would have been all too easy to conclude that the driver had made a mistake under such circumstances, but evidence to the contrary was supplied by the rear-facing camera mounted on the Williams. It revealed that the left rear suspension had broken, pitching the FW15C out of control.

This was a worrying development for the Williams camp. Earlier, during that same session, the mechanics had noticed that Prost's car had a cracked rear lower suspension wishbone. This was duly replaced, but now both cars were again both fitted with replacement lower rear suspension wishbones prior to the start of second qualifying.

Now Prost grabbed pole position ahead of Michael Schumacher's Benetton-Ford and Ayrton Senna's McLaren. Damon found himself pushed back to fourth place on the second row. 'I was disappointed not to have gone quicker on my second run,' he said, 'but the tyres just didn't seem to work as well and it never felt as though the car came good. But if I can get on the podium at the end of the race, then I will be delighted.'

Closer to victory. Damon leads Prost, and Senna's McLaren, in the opening phase of the 1993 Spanish Grand Prix at Barcelona. Only an engine failure came between Hill and a likely victory in this race.

Damon ahead again. Leading Alain once more over the first few laps of the 1993 Canadian Grand Prix at Montreal. This time Prost won again, with Damon third behind Michael Schumacher's Benetton.

Bette Hill was there in the pit lane which held so many fond, lingering memories amassed over so many years. 'I'm so proud of you,' she said, hugging her son. 'I know you are,' replied Damon, any self-consciousness concealed by helmet and balaclava. With admirable restraint, she'd done a dignified job not to smother him with excessive attention during his time in F1. But she deserved this moment almost as much as he did.

Come the start, Prost's Williams was moving ever so slightly before the green light flashed on, so although the Frenchman took an immediate lead, he was flagged in for a 10 second 'stop-go' penalty at the end of lap 11. That handed Schumacher a commanding lead which he retained through until lap 32 when he stopped out on the circuit with a hydraulic leak which prompted a minor fire in his Benetton's engine compartment.

Senna, who had bruised a wrist quite badly in a heavy shunt during practice, was adopting a softly-softly strategy, running steadily in third place from the start ahead of Hill. Damon's biggest problem for much of the afternoon was coping with the challenge posed by the Ferraris of Alesi and Berger, both of which got too close for comfort when the Englishman began to pick his way through traffic as he lapped the slower cars.

In truth, Damon was not getting through that slower traffic as decisively as he really needed to. On lap 28, yet again he found his fortunes resting in the hands of Alessandro Zanardi who proved more difficult to lap than Hill had expected. Damon later conceded this shortcoming.

'Yes,' he acknowleged. 'I must admit that throughout the race I was losing too much time in the traffic. That is part of learning Monaco, I think. I was very circumspect about taking chances to get through. But, really, the only way to get through sometimes is to muscle them out of the way – and I was very wary about doing that.

'I feel I lost more time than I should have done, particularly when I found myself behind Brundle and Andretti. They were too intent on their own race, and that allowed the Ferrari to catch up with me.'

When Schumacher retired, Senna found himself presented with a comfortable lead, and Damon alone was left as the only possible challenger to stand between the Brazilian and a record sixth Monaco Grand Prix victory.

Left *Head down and hard at it behind the wheel of the Williams-Renault FW15C.*

On lap 35 the Williams was 13.9 sec. behind the McLaren. It was as close as he was going to get. Five laps later he was 19.4 sec. down and drifted back to 27.4 sec. behind by lap 50, allowing Senna the luxury of a precautionary late stop for fresh tyres.

Ayrton emerged with a 9.4 sec. lead over Damon, so it was all over bar the shouting, and, with only eight of the race's 78 laps left to run, Gerhard Berger had hauled his Ferrari sufficiently close to Hill's Williams to convince him that he had a realistic chance of challenging for second place.

Going into the Loews hairpin Berger lunged for the inside, misjudged the manoeuvre and made smart contact with Damon's car. The impact spun the Williams across the nose of the Ferrari and Hill shuddered to a halt. With great presence of mind, however, he managed to prevent his Renault engine from stalling and successfully resumed the chase.

'There was no way I was going to leave him any more room,' said Damon, 'so I closed the door and he hit me. That spun us both round. I was fuming with anger and then, with my car parked across the road, no-one else could get through.

'I managed to get reverse, remarkably enough, and drive off, which he wasn't able to do. For the first few laps after I got that tap from him the car felt very unusual. I was concerned in those last seven laps that I could have another suspension failure.'

Hindsight is a gloriously beneficial commodity, but it's probably fair to say that Hill did as well as could be expected in his first serious crack at the Monaco Grand Prix. Despite his injured wrist, Senna's record through those streets has always been nothing short of formidable and, as the season wore on, the excellence of the McLaren MP4/8 technical package would become ever more apparent.

'It is 30 years since my father's first victory here and I'm sure he would have been the first to congratulate Ayrton on breaking his record of five wins,' said Damon.

'It is a tribute to my father as much as to him that it has taken someone of Ayrton's calibre to do it.' Senna could see that the words came from the heart. That Brazilian turned to him with a smile and shook his hand quietly. Damon hadn't simply been mouthing plati-

Main picture *Damon leading the 1993 British Grand Prix at Silverstone with Prost tight on his tail. Next time round Hill's engine would fail mightily.*

Inset *Hockenheim again – and Damon's luck runs true to his Formula 3000 form at the circuit near Heidelberg. Leading the 1993 German Grand Prix, a tyre failed with just over a lap left before the chequered flag.*

tudes and Ayrton appreciated that. It was a moment of genuine, spontaneous warmth.

Damon's six points for second place, allied to Schumacher's retirement, meant that he went back into second place in the drivers' championship points table as the Formula 1 circus upped sticks and headed across the Atlantic for its only race in North America, the Canadian Grand Prix.

It has to be recorded that the 1993 race at Montreal's Circuit Gilles Villeneuve was hardly foremost in the minds of local sports fans. The track may be named after the country's legendary, long-gone Grand Prix star, but the local populace was more concerned with the fact that the Montreal Canadiens had, that same week, triumphed in the final of the Stanley Cup, ice hockey's most prestigious competition.

. . . his afternoon fell apart when he made a routine tyre stop

This memorable success had taken place on the Wednesday evening prior to the race – after which drunken fans took the city centre apart. The Formula 1 action looked small beer by contrast.

Hill arrived at the circuit feeling optimistic about his chances – with some justification. 'At least I knew the way round before I started, and everything is really falling into place for me now,' he enthused.

'We are really benefiting from the electronic throttle system here because, on a track like this where you need to brake from high speed in sixth gear down to first gear a couple of times on each lap, the downchanges are much cleaner. You can concentrate totally on controlling the car.'

But Prost had the upper hand – firmly. He started ahead on Friday and sustained his advantage the following day. He qualified for pole with a lap time one full second faster than Hill could manage.

'Alain is good on this type of track,' said Damon. 'It's slow and very technical. He got more out of the conditions than I managed to do.'

The first three rows of the grid lined up Noah's Ark style. The two Williams, followed by the two Benettons (Schumacher and Patrese), followed by the two Ferraris (Berger and Alesi). Senna, frustrated by technical problems, could only qualify his McLaren seventh.

It proved to be a disappointing race for Hill. Although he led from the start, Prost neatly outbraked him into the first-gear hairpin at the far end of the circuit. As Alain steadily pulled clear, Damon had his hands full steadying his advantage over the hard-charging Senna who'd made up no fewer than four places on the opening lap alone.

Hill handled the pressure admirably, but his afternoon fell apart when he made a routine tyre stop at the end of lap 30. His Williams was stationary for an agonizing 16.3 sec. The Williams mechanics were on the point of fitting his replacement wheels when somebody noticed that they carried a set of tyres stencilled with Prost's race number.

Current regulations require that the seven sets of tyres allocated to each car per weekend must be marked with that car's number – anybody using an incorrectly marked tyre could face possible disqualification. The potential error was spotted in the nick of time, but Senna was now through into second place and, more seriously, had built up sufficient time to make a quick (5.05 sec.) tyre change himself next time round without losing his place back to Damon.

Hill was now fourth. Senna would subsequently retire, so Damon found himself promoted to third behind Prost and Schumacher at the chequered flag. Brushing aside any disappointment over that fumbled tyre change, he just said: 'I didn't find as much advantage on the new tyres as I thought I would have done. Also, the engine was sounding a little different towards the end, so I decided just to concentrate on getting the car to the finish.'

Still, he had clung on to his third place in the points table. Schumacher had closed the gap with that second place, but remained two points adrift as the circus returned to Europe for the meat of the summer season.

However, there was an uncomfortable tailpiece to the Canadian Grand Prix. The FISA technical delegate attending the race had reported that, in his view, the active suspension systems employed by several teams, did not conform to the current regulations.

In reality, this was a tactical move by the sport's governing body to signal that, come hell or high water, such esoteric accessories would not be permitted in 1994. And if the teams were not prepared to accept a rule change to that effect, then the systems would risk becoming outlawed immediately on the basis that they contravened the present rules.

In the context of this narrative, Formula 1 racing's latest domestic dispute has no specific bearing. But it should be recorded as an episode which put the Williams team understandably on the defensive. Frank and Patrick Head concluded that they'd become too successful. FISA was now seemingly prepared to stop at nothing to rein in their performance advantage. To say the least, it was an unsettling period.

By now, Damon's relationship with Alain Prost had eased into a comfortable, straightforward pattern. They got on well, if formally. Williams insiders reported that it was a no-nonsense situation with both men behaving in a mature, intelligent fashion towards each other. Not, you might say, a situation always to be found in top-line Grand Prix teams.

Preparing for action. Damon dons his balaclava while the helmet waits in the foreground.

'It is a professional relationship,' reflected Damon succinctly. 'You don't have to be friends with the people you work with, but you need to get on with them. You must create the right environment whereby you get the most out of yourself and don't create any animosity – unless that's the way you want to work, but I don't like working like that.

'I like Alain, but I wouldn't count him as a friend of mine. I wouldn't presume to. I want to find out how I match up against him on real terms.'

So, did Damon feel it was a relationship between master and pupil? Or an alliance of equals? 'Alain is under no obligation to help me. It's not his job. But if I want to know something, I'll ask him and he'll tell me. But I don't presume that he should help me in any way. Formula 1 is all about helping yourself.

'If I get stuck, I'll ask his advice. I'd be stupid if I didn't try to learn from Alain Prost.'

What had Prost taught him? 'Well, it's difficult to say specifically,' he pondered. 'It's just the way of working that I've learned from him. His concentration over a race weekend is total and he barely spends a second without thinking what needs to be done, or what can be done, to win the race.

'That makes it very hard work. He puts in a lot of hard work, mental concentration. That has not surprised me. Any moment you relax, you have to think, "Alain's not going to relax now." It's too late when you get into the car, you're five laps into the race and you think, "Oh, bugger, I should have done such-and-such."'

At the start of July 1993, F1 speculation was reaching fever pitch about the Williams team's possible strategy for the French and British Grands Prix. Respectively the home races for Prost and Hill, they would be held a week apart at Magny-Cours and Silverstone. If Alain won in France, so the stories went, Damon would be permitted to win at Silverstone.

Permitted to win. It was a phrase which could be taken both ways. On the face of it 'permitted to win' tended to down-grade Damon's contribution to the team effort. He'd been consistently quick in Silverstone testing, his confidence was running at an all-time high, and many observers seriously believed that he would genuinely be capable of giving Prost a run for his money on the wide open spaces of the former RAF base.

There was, however, a snag. On the Friday following the Silverstone race, the FISA World Council was scheduled to adjudicate on the legality of some fuel samples taken at earlier races. The jungle drums beat out the message that Prost's fuel from his winning run at Barcelona was not in conformity with the rules.

Acutely worried by these rumours, Williams was privately bracing itself for a disqualification from the Spanish Grand Prix – and if the light at the end of this particular tunnel did in fact turn out to be an oncoming train, could Prost, with the World Championship in mind, indulge the luxury of helping Hill to win at Silverstone?

First, though, there was the French Grand Prix. Damon delighted both himself and the team by qualifying for the first pole position of his career. Prost hit trouble early on the first morning, spinning off after only two laps because of a programming problem with the software controlling his car's anti-lock braking system.

As a result, he was stranded out on the circuit and never quite made up for that lost time. Hill ended the first day in an upbeat mood, but he wasn't underestimating Alain's potential for improvement.

Prost didn't use the ABS braking system on Saturday, but Damon retained it on his car. Hill's best Friday time had been 1 min. 15.051 sec. but he soon improved that to 1 min. 14.382 sec. to consolidate his position at the head of the field.

Prost replied with a 1 min. 14.911 sec. on his first run before retiring to the pit lane garage for a while, hoping for cooler conditions later in the session. With 15 minutes to go, he re-emerged on to the circuit – 1 min. 14.818 sec., 1 min. 14.564 sec., 1 min. 14.524 sec. On that final lap he'd been half a second quicker than Hill at the timing split mid-way round the lap, but squandered that advantage when he locked tyres coming into the final corner.

Damon tried to improve on his second run, but counted himself lucky to get away unscathed when he lightly collided with Michele Alboreto's Lola-Ferrari. And he knew he had been a lucky lad.

'The impact was hard enough to have broken a steering arm,' he admitted. 'Although I got away with it, the steering felt a little strange for the rest of the lap.'

His pole position was secure, nevertheless. 'I have made a big effort to concentrate and drive hard over the last few qualifying sessions,'

Scrambling through the chicane after the pits at Monza, just after passing Jean Alesi's Ferrari F93A, on the way to victory in the 1993 Italian Grand Prix – Damon's GP hat trick.

said Damon, 'and I rather feel that I have at last come out from behind Alain's shadow.'

Come the start of the race, it certainly looked that way. Hill made a barnstorming start to lead by 1.6 sec. from Prost at the end of the opening lap. Second time round it was 2.3 sec. but Alain trimmed it back to 2.1 sec. only for Damon to open it out again on lap four.

This was a two-horse race. By lap eight, the Williams-Renaults were 11.6 sec. ahead of Martin Brundle's Ligier in third place – despite both cars becoming coated with oil which was leaking from the rear of Japanese driver Ukyo Katayama's Tyrrell, already lapped following an early pit stop.

'He's physically powerful and if the car is bucking around a bit he's all right'

Hill led all the way to lap 27 when he came in for a 7.1 sec. tyre stop. Alain made a 6.94 sec. stop two laps later and just got back on the circuit ahead of his team-mate.

'As I came into the pit lane I found myself following Michael Andretti's McLaren,' explained Damon, 'and I got boxed in behind him again as we accelerated out. Then, as we came up to the end of the pit lane at full chat, one of the Saubers was waved out in front of us and there was very nearly a big accident.

'That delayed me enough that Alain was able to rejoin ahead of me. We had a good dice from then on. I gave some serious thought to making a second stop to change tyres, but the risk factor would have been too high. As we didn't have to push too hard, I stayed out.'

At the end of the race, Alain led Damon across the line by 0.3 sec. to score the Williams team's first 1-2 finish of the season. They had buried the opposition and played to the crowd. But what would happen in seven days time?

'Don't ask me questions like that,' said Prost at the post-race press conference. 'I will obviously be very happy if Damon can win his home Grand Prix at Silverstone, as I did here today, but I must think about the Championship.'

On the other hand, in the run-up to the Silverstone race, Patrick Head was credited with a telling remark. 'I think it's fairly clear that we were asking Damon to support Alain in this race and I think it will be slightly different at Silverstone.'

That sent *Autosport* into top gear. The cover of their preview issue proclaimed: 'British Grand Prix – Why Damon can win' and continued to quote more from the Williams Technical Director.

'We have difficulty getting the active suspension to behave in a way that's good for that circuit,' he said. 'It can sometimes make it tough to drive. It's the same problem we had at Barcelona. Damon was quite happy there and would have won the race if his engine hadn't gone.

'I think the British Grand Prix is going to be difficult for us and I would put a few bob on Damon. He's physically powerful and if the car is bucking around a bit he's all right. At Silverstone our car needs a firm hand, a bit more brutal than maybe Alain is.'

The Williams team collectively put on hold its concern over the outcome of the following week's FISA World Council meeting and buckled down to the challenge of Silverstone. For Damon, however, things didn't get off on a very positive note.

Torrential rain lashed the circuit on Friday morning and, after only four laps of the free practice session, he dumped his Williams into the sand trap at Stowe corner. He'd set fastest time by then – and it remained fastest for the whole session. Not that this was of any significance, because few cars went out.

'I wouldn't want to have to race in those conditions,' he shrugged. 'I just hit the brakes going into Stowe at 130 mph and locked up. From then on there was nothing I could do.'

In the afternoon, when it mattered, Alain was commandingly quickest. The World Championship points leader managed a 1 min. 34.483 sec. best, Damon only managing a time some 1.8 sec. slower after being balked by slower cars on his best run on a track surface which was drying all the time.

On the first lap of Hill's crucial second run he was 0.6 sec. ahead of Prost at the first timing split on the Hangar Straight. The bottom line was a 1 min. 19.637 sec. lap. Damon then further improved to 1 min. 19.134 sec. which really set Prost on his mettle.

With BBC television's Murrary Walker hooked into Hill's car on the team radio link, it was only to be expected that the commentator would whip himself up into a frenzied state of excitement when

Inset *After starting from the back of the grid at Estoril, Damon stormed through the field to finish third in the Portuguese Grand Prix. Here he positions himself inside Barrichello's Jordan in pursuit of Johnny Herbert's Lotus* and **Main picture** *completes the manoeuvre decisively during his magnificent recovery.*

Damon posted fastest time. He was already trumpeting that Hill had decisively bagged the fastest time, when Prost popped up with a stunning 1 min. 19.006 sec. with five minutes left to claim the 28th pole position of his career!

Patrick Head was left grinning fit to bust. 'That's what it should all be about,' he enthused. 'Two guys getting really stuck in and giving each other a bit of stick.' Nobody was about to argue with that.

What was clear, however, was that Silverstone 1993 would not produce the hysterical Mansell-mania which sparked the post-race track invasion after Mansell's victory the previous year. The insurance implications of this mindless disregard for safety had sent the circuit owners into an understandable state of shock.

'I feel anger, a furious sense of disbelief. You do everything right and something stops you'

From the standpoint of public safety – not to mention insurance considerations – Silverstone just couldn't risk a repeat of such chaotic scenes. Over £80,000 had been spent on improving spectator security prior to the 1993 British Grand Prix. But they needn't have worried.

In the event, a modest crowd of 60,000 turned out on race day, making a three-day total barely half that of the 200,000 plus attendance the previous year. Silverstone didn't like that, but they grinned and beared it. The dyed-in-the-wool motor racing fans – who don't, it has to be said, have to foot the bill for staging the race – received an unexpected bonus in terms of easy access and an uncrowded environment in which to relish their sport.

And enjoy it they did – for 41 of the 59 laps at any rate. From second place on the grid, Damon burst into an immediate lead on the sprint down to Copse Corner. At the same time, Senna rocketed into second place, cutting off Prost from challenging the Englishman on his home ground.

Hill came barnstorming through at the end of the opening lap 1.4 sec. ahead of Senna, the Brazilian pulling every trick in the book to keep the other Williams behind his McLaren. Even by Ayrton's own standards, the aggressively defensive manner in which he held off his old rival attracted frowns from everyone including his most ardent supporters. He was well over the top and it took every ounce of Prost's concentration – and eight laps' endeavour – to find a gap through which he could squeeze to take over second place.

Damon was now 8.1 sec. ahead and driving immaculately. Everybody was now hypnotized by the gap separating the two Williams-Renaults. Hill's advantage fluttered – 8.2 sec., 7.8 sec., 8.0 sec., 7.6 sec. By lap 28 Prost had chiselled his way to within 5.2 sec. of the Englishman but, with the routine tyre stops beckoning, the outcome still looked as though it could go either way.

On lap 29 Prost came in for tyres. He was stationary for 8.02 sec. Next time round Hill was serviced in 7.96 sec. But, just as the previous weekend, Alain made the best of his breaks in traffic and the two cars picked up the threads of their battle only 3.3 sec. apart.

By lap 35 Alain was only 1.3 sec. adrift and it looked as though the race might be slipping away from Damon at last. But catching Hill was one thing; passing him would be quite another.

Suddenly, out came the safety car and the pack closed up into tight formation. Luca Badoer's slow Lola-Ferrari had rolled to a standstill on the outside of Woodcote, so the stewards deemed – questionably – that everyone should be slowed up while marshals moved the abandoned car out of the possible line of fire.

After three laps 'cruising', the green flag was shown and Hill immediately picked up a 1.3 sec. advantage. Prost pulled him back again but, just as it seemed as though the Williams teamsters were about to lock horns seriously for the lead, Damon's engine expired dramatically and he rolled to a halt.

Prost cruised the remaining 18 laps to an easy win, the 50th of his career, but he had a keen appreciation of the crowd's disappointment, and hardly acknowledged the chequered flag as he came out of Woodcote for the last time.

Hill, who stopped off for a beer at the British Racing Drivers' Club enclosure on his walk back to the paddock, just shrugged.

'In situations like this, you just feel empty,' he said. 'It's only the second time this year that one of our engines has blown up, and both times it has cost me a race. I feel anger, a furious sense of disbelief. You do everything right and something stops you . . .'

Prost was acutely sensitive about the whole situation. 'I don't really

In heavy traffic, Ayrton Senna's McLaren and Alain Prost's Williams are already out of sight through the first corner of the Japanese Grand Prix at Suzuka as Mika Hakkinen's McLaren heads the rest of the pack. Hill is sixth behind Gerhard Berger's Ferrari (28) and Michael Schumacher's Benetton (5) with Eddie Irvine's Jordan right on the tail of the German driver.

like winning in this ambience,' he confessed. 'I think Damon deserved to win here at home, but I also think I did a good job today.'

Prost also wondered whether Damon had been running his engine a little harder, perhaps pulling a few more revs than he had been using. His remark was wrongly construed as implying that perhaps Damon had been, in some small part, the architect of his own downfall.

In fact, that certainly wasn't the case. Renault Sport's genial Chief Engineer, Bernard Dudot, moved quickly to quell any such speculation. 'Neither of our drivers so much as touched their rev limiters all afternoon,' he asserted. 'Damon's engine let go suddenly and no way was it his fault. He was superb, and we're all very disappointed for him.'

When the engines were stripped down at Renault Sport's technical base at Viry-Chatillon, near Paris, Damon's was found to have suffered a broken exhaust valve. It had been 'Just One of Those Things'.

Damon quickly came to terms with this disappointment. The one thing his time at Williams had taught him to be was a team player. That can sometimes be a difficult task for a Grand Prix driver, subordinating his own personal ambitions to the good of the team as a whole.

Already approaching the season's halfway point, there had been rumours surfacing to the effect that Hill was being somehow constrained by team orders. In the early part of the year, it would have been difficult to grant these rumours much credibility. Damon's inexperience was such that he wasn't really capable of running with Prost. Not consistently, at any rate.

However, from the French Grand Prix onwards, things looked rather different. Damon was picking up the pace. In reality, it would always be difficult to judge how hard Prost was pushing – perhaps just hard enough to keep a wafer-thin advantage over his colleague – but there could be no doubting that Hill was coming to grips with front-line Formula 1 to the point where he was a contender.

'Alain always goes just as fast as he needs to,' says Frank Williams, reflecting on the 1993 season. But if Alain was driving tactically, by the same token, how much more was there to come from Damon if he was put under even greater pressure?

Away from the pit lane the next fortnight would bring mixed fortunes for the Williams team. The FISA World Council did not, as anticipated, find that the fuel samples from previous races contravened the regulations. On the other hand, a marathon meeting of the F1 constructors on the eve of first practice for the German Grand Prix at Hockenheim still left them frustrated over the shape of the 1994 technical regulations.

The message from the sport's governing body was stark. In effect, you can keep your active suspension and traction control systems, and all the other electronic gizmos, until the end of 1993 – and then they are banned. You can keep arguing, if you like, but they will be banned. Period.

Damon was bristling with the sort of controlled indignation for which his late father was renowned

---

Damon had spent much of his two years as Williams's test driver helping to develop such systems, but in the second half of July 1993 he had more pressing matters on his mind – like winning his first Grand Prix.

During practice at Hockenheim, Damon found himself shoved off the road and into a sand trap by Michele Alboreto, the Italian whose Lola-Ferrari he'd collided with during practice at Magny-Cours. This time, however, Damon was bristling with the sort of controlled indignation for which his late father was renowned.

He marched down to Alboreto's pit lane garage and gave his adversary a piece of his mind. Michele, one of the nicest men you could wish to meet, in effect told Damon that he thought it was his own bloody fault and couldn't care less. With his own Grand Prix career crumbling round his ears, Alboreto, who'd won the German Grand Prix for Ferrari eight years earlier, had other things to worry about than the plaintive objections of a man lucky enough to be driving the best car in the business!

Qualifying on this high-speed circuit through the pine forests near Heidelberg saw Prost on pole ahead of Hill, but for the third successive race it was Damon who made the best start to lead through the first corner. Michael Schumacher's Benetton was in second place ahead of Prost and, as they braked for the tricky Ostkurve chicane at

Damon really had to work hard in the early stages of the 1993 Japanese race after qualifying on the third row of the grid. Here he lines up Schumacher's Benetton and (below) Berger's Ferrari.

the far end of the circuit, Alain glanced in his mirrors to see Martin Brundle's Ligier starting to spin right behind him!

Prost duly steered up the chicane escape road to avoid the pirouetting Ligier which duly followed his example, both cars rejoining without any drama. But Alain, after carving through to take the lead from Damon on the eighth lap, found himself cruelly rewarded for his quick thinking by receiving his second 'stop-go' penalty of the season.

That handed Damon what should have been a clear run through to victory, for both Williams drivers were confident that they could run non-stop to the finish without changing tyres. Alain could do little more than nibble into Damon's advantage in the second half of the race, there being no way he could make up sufficient ground to win after his earlier heartache.

By lap 39 of the 45 lap race Prost had closed to within 11 sec. Damon asked over the radio link, 'One-two, or two-one?' – meaning, did he have to relinquish the lead to Alain? He was reassured by a board from his pit crew which read 'P1 OK.' It was to be his race, at last.

In the media room, I picked up the telephone and rang the sports desk at *The Guardian*. The entire British press corps were mentally sharpening their wits. It was 31 years since Graham Hill had won this same race on a rain-soaked Nürburgring. Five laps to go. Four, three, two . . .

Coming out of the Ostkurve for the penultimate time Damon's heart jumped as he noticed the puncture warning light flickering on his Williams dashboard.

'Initially I wasn't too worried, because sometimes it comes on if you are pushing very hard because the tyre pressures have dropped a bit,' he later recalled.

'I then felt the car oversteer suddenly as I came out of the chicane, but I was in fourth gear, accelerating up towards 130 mph when the left rear tyre suddenly went. It must have been a sharp object – or something like that – going right through the tyre . . .'

His Williams slowed to near-walking pace, its left rear wheel rim trailing shards of rubber. Just like Nigel Mansell at Adelaide in 1986 when the World Championship slipped from his grasp. Prost went through to notch up his 51st Grand Prix victory.

How long would Damon Hill have to wait for that elusive first victory?

The answer, of course, was three weeks precisely. All of which returns us to where we came in, beneath the blazing skies at the Hungaroring, near Budapest.

There was one fascinating tailpiece to his maiden Grand Prix victory. Ayrton Senna, whose McLaren had been chasing him hard in the opening stages, retired out on the circuit after only 17 of the 77 laps. Rather than hurry back to the pits, the Brazilian watched from the trackside.

Damon later said he was trying to be particularly neat and tidy on this section of the circuit, mindful that the Great Man seemed to be sizing him up.

In the light of what was to happen over the next three months, one wonders whether Damon was closer to the truth than even he might have known. Or was Senna displaying an uncanny degree of prescience?

After the French Grand Prix, Damon had retained his third place in the Drivers' World Championship points stakes, but those disappointments at Silverstone and Hockenheim saw Michael Schumacher overtake him again.

In Hungary, however, Schumacher's Benetton failed to finish, so Damon's victory vaulted him back two points ahead of the young German star. Everybody in the Williams team was absolutely delighted that their 'baby' had finally broken his duck. Frank Williams even ventured the opinion that now Damon had won his first race, he would probably win the next two or three!

On the face of it, this seemed like an over-optimistic prediction, but there is certainly some historic evidence from which one can conclude that winning a first Grand Prix is the most difficult of all. Nigel Mansell took nearly six years before he made it to the F1 winner's circle – and immediately scored his second win at the very next race!

History was about to repeat itself.

Pressure. How to handle pressure. Unlock the answer to that conun-

Above *Immersed in thought prior to the start of the final race in the 1993 World Championship. Third place at Adelaide dropped him to third in the final points table behind Ayrton Senna who won the race on his last outing for McLaren.*

Right *His father's son. Even the sideburns are pure 1970s, just like the Old Man's!*

drum and you've successfully found the answer to one, just one, of the many challenges facing any professional sportsman. And in winning his first Grand Prix, Damon Hill had successfully proved that he could handle that fickle commodity. The pressure of running free from pressure.

'It is a factor,' he had admitted on the afternoon before that historic first win. 'The pressure in Formula 1 is immense. You could walk across a plank if it was three inches wide and two feet above the ground. But if it was two hundred feet up, you're not going to be able to do it. Why not? It's the same plank. But you've got to forget you're two hundred feet up!

'I'm very keen to build on that first win and score some more successes'

'Certainly, when you're in the car, you don't allow yourself to think of anything else. But the easiest thing is to become distracted. There are certainly tricks you can play to make yourself concentrate.

'For example, Nigel Mansell was criticized a few times last year for putting in fastest laps close to the end of the race, but that's one good way of making yourself concentrate.

'The greatest risk is lack of concentration, rather than the making of a mistake because you are driving too fast.'

Confidence breeds confidence. In Damon Hill's case, that would become immediately apparent on the first day of qualifying for the Belgian Grand Prix at Spa-Francorchamps. Revelling in the sense of enhanced self-belief engendered by his win at Budapest, Damon set fastest time in the first qualifying session on that challenging 4.213-mile circuit which threads a spectacular path through the pine forests close to the German border.

'I was quite relieved to get that first win out of the way,' admitted Damon, 'so now I can knuckle down and perhaps be a little more aggressive about my whole approach. I've come here with the firm intention of trying to win the race. I'm very keen to build on that first win and score some more successes.

'I feel a lot more comfortable about things. After today's session I actually felt quite happy, rather than totally stressed-out as I did in the past. I think that is part of the pay-off from that first win!'

One of the first to congratulate Hill on his achievement was a man who knows all about success at Spa. It was his namesake Phil Hill, the 66-year-old Californian who won the 1961 World Championship and that year's Belgian Grand Prix on the old eight-mile Spa road circuit.

Phil had been an old friend and colleague of Damon's father and had a close bond with his late colleague's son. In the immediate aftermath of Graham's death Damon spent a few weeks in California staying with Hill and his wife Alma at their Santa Monica home. The idea was to get the lad away and enable him to gather his thoughts.

During that time he'd worked as an odd-job man for some of his spell away, helping at Phil's car restoration company as well as sweeping the floors at All American Racers – the Santa Ana-based racing team owned by Phil and Graham's friend and rival, Dan Gurney.

Gurney, who'd been Graham Hill's team-mate in the BRM squad during a troubled 1960 season, remembered this interlude in a letter to the author early in 1994:

My recollection of Damon at that time was one of a young man in shock, a young man who was asking such questions as 'what is life all about?' The fact was that Graham was no longer with us. I don't know how one learns to cope with it, but that is what Damon was going through. I don't think any of us are equipped to deal with anything as sudden or final as that.

I think he spent some time with my oldest son John, and I think he was looking for essentially something to take his mind off the recent events, if at all possible, so he was a young man in a trance to some degree. I'm sure he didn't know what he wanted to do in life at that time. He showed a lot of the same natural curiosity and adventuresome spirit that both his mother and father demonstrated many times in the past.

They say that time gradually heals the wounds that come from such a tragedy. I'm sure that the process continues to this day for all of those who were touched by it.

I know his mother Bette, and Georgie, his wife, are very proud of

Speak up Ayrton, you're through! Williams Commercial Director Richard West wrestling with the Brazilian phone system as he attempts to make contact with the team's new driver at a media conference held at Didcot in late 1993. Damon looks on pensively.

Damon is on hand to celebrate the 1994 Williams driver line-up in company with Frank W. Nobody could have seen how tragically short-lived it would be.

him. Graham would have felt the same way. The family tradition lives on. I even caught a glimpse of that famous sense of humour recently!

Practice for the Belgian Grand Prix provided the Formula 1 fraternity with one of those periodic reminders that mator racing is dangerous. Lotus driver Alessandro Zanardi crashed horrifyingly on the fast Eau Rouge corner at over 150 mph during Friday morning's untimed session. He was sufficiently shaken not to take any further part in the weekend's proceedings, but everybody agreed it had been a close shave.

Second qualifying saw Hill 0.9 sec. behind Prost to take second place on the grid, but when Damon was fastest in the race morning warm-up, things were looking good for the Englishman.

Prost had now mastered the starting technique demanded of the Williams FW15C and made a copybook getaway to take an immediate lead into the tight La Source hairpin. Senna also made a terrific getaway in his McLaren and ran round the outside of Hill to take second place as the cars disappeared down the hill, over the Eau Rouge bridge and off into the country.

By the end of the opening lap Alain slammed past the pits a whopping 2.8 sec. ahead of Senna. Damon was closing in on the McLaren and, on the 195 mph drag up the long straight beyond Eau Rouge, he popped out of Senna's slipstream and cleanly out-braked the Brazilian going into the Les Combes ess-bends.

By the end of eight laps, Prost was 4.5 sec. ahead of Hill but, with two scheduled tyre stops on the agenda, the pendulum could swing either way. By the end of the first round of tyre stops Damon had closed the gap to Prost from 6.1 sec. on lap 14 to 0.9 sec. on lap 21. Then came the second round of tyre changes, and Damon took full tactical advantage of being the first of the two Williams drivers to make his stop.

On lap 29 of the 44-lap race, Damon came in for a 6.1 sec. change. Next time round Alain appeared in the pit lane, but a sticking front wheel nut and the need to wait for one of the Saubers to accelerate past, meant that he was at a standstill for 9.11 sec.

Waved back into the battle, Alain found himself accelerating hard down the pit lane as Damon came slamming into the braking area for the La Source hairpin. The pit lane exits on to the circuit just after that right corner and, as Prost steered his Williams back on to the track, Damon powered past to take the lead in the Belgian Grand Prix.

By his own admission, Prost had been a couple of laps behind schedule making his second tyre stop and, on his final set of rubber, he felt the fine edge of his Williams's handling had been lost. He couldn't quite get through Eau Rouge without slightly feathering the throttle – and that was all that the third-placed Michael Schumacher needed to take a run at him on the gentle, yet blindingly fast, climb to Les Combes.

On lap 32 the Benetton-Ford driver successfully demoted Prost from second place and set out after Damon with a vengeance. Even allowing for the Williams's power advantage, Damon might have been excused had he made a slip under such pressure. But he didn't.

'whatever team I'm with, I will be trying to get the very best from the machinery'

In the 12 laps remaining Hill never put a wheel wrong, and made it to the chequered flag with a 3.88 sec. cushion over the gallant Schumacher, with Prost hanging on to finish a strong third. Damon was ecstatic!

'Once I was ahead it was just a question of pushing as hard as I could, and since I was already driving at 100 per cent it was fantastic,' he explained. 'After Hungary, this race felt like the equivalent of five laps there. It went by in a flash!'

It was perhaps somehow appropriate that Damon's success not only marked the 50th win for a Renault-powered Grand Prix car, but it also clinched the Williams team's sixth Constructors' World Championship title. His place was secure in the Williams line-up for 1994. Wasn't it?

His recent success notwithstanding, rumours began to circulate in the run-up to the Italian Grand Prix that Damon might just conceivably be replaced by Ayrton Senna in the Williams squad for 1994. The word was that Rothmans, who were taking over as the Williams title sponsor the following year, wanted the F1 super-team of all time. Senna and Prost.

Yet we were all looking in the wrong direction. We should have known that, when Prost intimated earlier in the year that there was no way he would drive alongside Senna again, the Frenchman meant it.

Curiously, Damon didn't seem to be too worried when he spoke on the eve of second practice at Monza.

'Frank Williams has an option on my services next year,' he said firmly, 'but he's told me he won't be talking about that until after the drivers' championship is settled.

'I would like to win a third Grand Prix, but Frank can sack me if he wants and I'll be happy to settle for three wins. It wouldn't be the end of the world. I've had a fantastic opportunity this year with Williams and, while I think they will continue to be the team to beat next year, whatever team I'm with, I will be trying to get the very best from the machinery.'

There spoke an extremely confident driver, or so it seemed. What we didn't really appreciate, of course, was that Prost's thoughts were already turning towards retirement. Hill must have worked it all out. It wasn't likely that he would be replaced, but perhaps more possible that Alain would call it a day – letting in Senna.

Damon again qualified second to Prost at Monza, but while Alain was quick off the mark once more, Hill got slightly bogged down in the run to the first chicane and found himself sitting it out with Senna's McLaren for the racing line. He didn't budge an inch, with the result that Ayrton was tossed over the Williams's left rear wheel and both cars survived unscheduled detours on to the run-off areas. They continued unscathed, completing the first lap in eighth and ninth places.

Victory for Prost at Monza would clinch his fourth World Championship title, and it now seemed as though he was left with an easy run to the chequered flag. Damon got his head down, tore back into contention, consolidating a strong second place as the race moved into its final stages.

Williams team orders reputedly called for the drivers to hold position over the last 10 laps – Damon was only 4.3 sec. adrift at the crucial lap 43 cut-off point, so Alain could now ease up. Hill drew right up into his wheeltracks only for his pit to hang out a signal read-

Right *Reflecting on his first year in a top team – and pondering, perhaps, about what the future may bring.*

ing 'TEMP. SLOW' to remind him he ought to watch his instruments.

What did this mean? Damon said later that the only factor preventing him from overtaking Prost was a slight loss of power from his overheating engine. Prost, on the other hand, explained that he was just taking things easy.

'I knew I had nothing to fear from Damon, because whoever was in front going into the last 10 laps was going to win,' he said. 'I was running my engine about 700 rpm down from its maximum and not pushing at all.'

This time, however, it was Alain's turn for the bad luck. With only five laps to go, his Renault engine expired spectacularly and he rolled to a halt out on the circuit at the Parabolica corner. Damon was thus left to come storming home to his third successive win. It also opened the tantalizing, if outside, mathematical possibility that Damon could win the Championship himself.

'I'm not even allowing myself to think about the Championship implications of this race,' said Damon cautiously, but I am delighted to have won my third successive Grand Prix. When Frank Williams told me after the Hungarian race that I could go on and probably win the next two, I did not really think it was likely. But it is like a dream come true, and I am delighted!'

First practice day at Estoril in preparation for the Portuguese Grand Prix, and everything began to fall into place. Prost announced he was retiring – and Senna announced he was leaving McLaren. Although there was no formal confirmation, the direct consequences of those public statements were now obvious. Ayrton Senna was to join Williams to run alongside Damon Hill in 1994.

Damon, however, kept his head down and did brilliantly well in Saturday's qualifying session to take the second pole position of his career. Prost, who encountered some problems – including a spin into the retaining wall – briefly tried Damon's car to see if it felt better than his own, but he could not get closer than 1.1 sec. away from his best time the previous day.

Hill's outside chance of the Drivers' World Championship ended

when he had problems firing up his Williams immediately prior to the parade lap, as a result of which he was late away and had to start the race from the back of the grid. Exactly as Prost had done at Hungaroring.

'The external starter became dislodged on Damon's car,' explained Patrick Head, 'and we had some difficulty inserting it back into its aperture because of the failure of a little light bulb inside the shaft which is designed to help the mechanics locate the correct position.

'Eventually we got the engine fired up, but it was still quite cold and running rather erratically. In a couple more seconds it would have been revving freely, but Damon flicked it into first gear and it stalled. By the time we reset the automatic gearchange and fired it up for the second time, the rest of the field was setting out on its parade lap.'

'I think you'd have to have mixed emotions about driving alongside someone of the power of Ayrton because he's fiercely competitive'

Jean Alesi led from the start, challenged by Senna's McLaren. In the end, however, Prost found himself chasing Schumacher for victory and, after his very firm challenge for the lead was thwarted by the German driver, Alain opted to play safe and clinch the title with second place.

Damon once again drove a stormer of a race. The last time he had been at the back of an F1 starting grid was at Silverstone the previous year, driving the old Brabham-Judd. That time he stayed last. But on this occasion he scythed through the pack to such dramatic effect that he was knocking on the door of the top six with only 15 of the race's 71 laps completed.

At the end of the day he finished third, less than 5 sec. behind Schumacher and Prost who crossed the line 0.9 sec. apart. 'My father once said that you meet a much nicer class of people at the back of the grid, but I won't say I agree with that,' grinned Hill.

'It was pretty fraught at times, but nevertheless very enjoyable. Naturally, I had a car advantage which helped me slide through a few people, but once I had completed about 15 laps, they spread out a bit more and it was very difficult to find a place to overtake.

'I had nothing to lose, which is sometimes quite a relief, so I could just go for it and drove as fast as I could. I am very pleased for Alain and want to congratulate him on his Championship.'

In the break between the Portuguese and Japanese Grands Prix, the Williams team held a press conference at Didcot. It was, in effect, formal confirmation of the Senna/Hill partnership for 1994. While Damon sat alongside Frank Williams in front of the assembled media, Williams Commercial Director Richard West struggled to get through to Ayrton in Sao Paulo on a specially arranged open phone link.

While the wonders of modern communications were explored, Damon gave his opinion on the prospect of driving with Senna: 'I think you'd have to have mixed emotions about driving alongside someone of the power of Ayrton because he's fiercely competitive. But, nevertheless, I expect to learn quite a lot from him. It's a pretty obvious challenge for any racing driver, and a challenge which I welcome. I'm sure I'll be up to it.'

How did he feel life would be when it came to working with Senna? Would it be more difficult than with Prost? Damon concealed a weary flicker of his eyebrows as he attempted to answer these predictable enquiries.

'The job of a racing driver is not only confined to circulating around the track,' he replied. 'As a driver, I know that in order to get where I want I have to work for the team and within the team. Ayrton has a reputation for getting what he wants out of a team, so that might be to my detriment.

'It may well be [a less easy relationship than with Prost] but I don't want to pre-judge it. I really don't know Ayrton terribly well. I've spoken to him a few times and raced him very little, really. But, put it this way; I'm looking forward to it. I know it's going to be a very exciting year.

'I think he [Ayrton] is far and away the most complete and the fastest driver currently racing – or will be when Alain retires. He's head and shoulders, really, above everybody else.'

However, Hill did make it crystal clear that he wasn't going to be intimidated by Ayrton's presence. 'I'm not easily demoralized or crushed,' he grinned, 'so I'm well prepared for that. I'm still on an upward climb in my F1 career and still have a lot to learn. Having someone like Ayrton as a team-mate will only add to my development.'

By this time, West was through to Senna in Brazil and everybody was queueing up to ask him whether he felt Damon might be a serious title contender. Senna's answer was a masterpiece of diplomatic evasion, bearing in mind that the Brazilian considers himself to be The Best.

'First of all, I think Damon is a different driver than he was when the Championship started, or put it this way, at this same time last year,' said Ayrton with that surgical brand of English linguistic mastery which always seems to take one's breath away.

'He has now almost a full season of experience; he has won Grands Prix, he has been on pole position and he has led races. He has forced his way up in a natural way which gives all of us drivers a lot of confidence. And I believe that for the next year, naturally, he will be a lot more competitive right away from the very first race, which is an important thing for the Championship.

'He couldn't have had a better start [to his F1 career] than one season with Alain and then a second season with me.'

Damon's victory at Monza had moved him into second place in the Drivers' World Championship stakes and, with Senna retiring both there and at Estoril, he went into the penultimate round of the title chase nine points ahead of the Brazilian.

However, Damon's maiden outing at Suzuka, venue for the Japanese Grand Prix, saw his qualifying efforts thwarted by acute disappointment. Mid-way through the second qualifying session, Hill managed to set fastest time – only to spin off under braking for the hairpin and hit a tyre barrier.

That ended his challenge for a front row starting position and he watched in frustration as Prost, Senna, Mika Hakkinen (McLaren), Schumacher and Gerhard Berger's Ferrari all went quicker, pushing him down to an eventual sixth place on the grid.

The race itself started in the dry, but was dramatically punctuated by a torrential rain shower from which Senna emerged with the upper hand over Prost. Damon, meanwhile, completed the opening in seventh place, overtaking Schumacher for sixth three laps into the contest and then fixing Berger firmly in his sights.

At the end of lap seven, Berger, Hill and Schumacher arrived in the braking area for the tight chicane before the pits in nose-to-tail formation. As Damon attempted to run down the outside of the Ferrari, Schumacher saw what he thought was his chance and dived up the inside, but locked up his front left tyre and slide into the Williams's right rear.

Schumacher was out on the spot with broken suspension, but Hill escaped apparently unscathed. Frustratingly, he was then forced into the pits to change a punctured tyre on lap 19, but was back a couple of laps later for rain tyres when the heavens opened.

This unfortunate sequence of events dropped him back to seventh, but he made the audacious decision to switch back to slicks on lap 28, with the wet track only just beginning to dry, and dropped back again from fourth to seventh.

'There was nothing wrong with the way Eddie drove as far as I was concerned'

He now faced an unexpected challenge from no less a rival than his old Formula 3000 sparring partner Eddie Irvine, the Ulsterman who was making his Grand Prix debut in the second Jordan-Hart 193. At this stage of the race, Irvine was still on rain tyres and harried Damon mercilessly as they jousted over sixth place.

Then, at the height of their battle, race leader Senna came storming up behind them in his McLaren MP4/8 – and was not amused by Irvine's reluctance to let him through. For several laps, Senna watched with mounting frustration as Irvine dropped wheels over the kerbs and threw dirt all over him and, in the process, causing the Brazilian's lead over Prost to shrink from 25 to 10 sec.

Eventually Senna found a way past and won convincingly from Prost, Mika Hakkinen and Damon. The Jordans of Barrichello and Irvine came home fifth and sixth, but that wasn't the end of the matter in Senna's mind, and he sought out Irvine for a tense confrontation a couple of hours after the race had ended.

Faced with a total lack of contrition on the part of the Ulsterman, Senna's temper ran out of control and he aimed a blow at the F1 newcomer, striking him on the side of the face.

Interestingly, Hill stood up for Irvine. 'There was nothing wrong with the way Eddie drove as far as I was concerned,' he said. 'The era

*The ultimate test? Damon with
Ayrton Senna at Estoril on the
official announcement of the
Williams team's multi-million
pound Rothmans sponsorship deal
for 1994.*

of one driver saying "after you Claude" is long gone and that is as much due to Senna as anybody else. He started being very aggressive when he came in and everybody else has copied him.'

This was a bold stance for Damon to take, knowing that he would be partnering Ayrton in 1994. He, the Englishman, did not shy away from repeating his opinion at the pole position press conference after practice for the Australian Grand Prix in Adelaide a fortnight later.

Asked if he felt Irvine was being unfair in his driving – and with Ayrton sitting alongside him – Damon attempted to defuse any tension by saying: 'I don't want to get involved in this, to be honest.'

Then he added: 'It was unfortunate that Eddie and I were racing for position. I was on slicks and he was on wets and Ayrton just happened to be lapping us at the same time.

'It's a very difficult situation. I can imagine how Ayrton felt, because I've led races and I know what it's like to get in trouble with backmarkers. On the other hand, Eddie was taking every opportunity to get past and I thought I would get away from him on slicks if I had a chance.

'So I didn't want to be behind him, but it's irritating for Ayrton, and I can see that. But a lot of people thought it was great to watch, and I enjoyed racing with Eddie, so I don't know what the answer is.'

Going into that final race, Damon was now only two points ahead of Senna in the battle for second place in the Championship. In Adelaide, Ayrton proved to be in a class of his own, qualifying the Ford V8-engined McLaren on pole position for the first time that season, and simply vanishing into the distance when the starting lights flickered to green.

Damon came home third behind Prost – and dropped to third in the final points tally, four behind Senna. He half-spun in the closing stages of the race as he made a vain bid to outbrake Alain for second place, but was broadly satisfied with the final race of his first season for the Williams team.

Looking back on the 1993 season, Damon had done everything and more that could have been expected of him. 'His outstanding characteristic is a fierce determination,' said Patrick Head. 'He seemed to have great depths of personal resource. Instead of wringing his hands and gnashing his teeth when things go wrong, he will sit down, go through the available data, work it all out and go quicker the next day.

'At Adelaide, for example, he had some problems on the first day of practice and then bounced back to be the fastest car on the second day. That was very impressive – and he did it a number of times. I was also impressed by the fact that, only if he was in desperation would he look over at Alain's chassis settings.

'Damon's ability level hasn't stabilized yet. He's learning, learning, learning . . . He's won three Grands Prix, which is one more than Michael Schumacher, and in truth could have won twice that number.

'I really believe that's a pretty impressive performance in a first year.'

Off-season testing provided disappointment for Hill in the form of two big shunts at Estoril in the immediate aftermath of the 1993 season. On both occasions he was testing the new 'passive' suspension systems in preparation for the new 1994 regulations, and on both occasions the cars were very badly damaged. But while the first of those accidents was probably down to driver error, the second was almost certainly because of car malfunction, and Damon successfully shrugged aside his disappointment.

'I believe I will start the coming season with a very good chance of the title'

After a winter holiday in the Caribbean with Georgie and the boys, Damon reappeared at Estoril in mid-January for the formal unveiling of the new Rothmans partnership and livery. Ayrton was also present and Damon seemed upbeat about the team's potential.

It was perhaps inevitable that the assembled press corps would ask Damon what he felt about the prospects of partnering a triple World Champion with a reputation of grinding his team-mate's nose into the tarmac.

Hill was defiantly positive in his response. 'What do people think Ayrton is going to do to me?' he enquired. 'Apply a Vulcan mind grip, or something? I appreciate that Ayrton is the benchmark for all F1 drivers, but there a number who think they can beat him.

'I believe I will start the coming season with a very good chance of

173

Same car, new paint job. Damon tests the Williams-Renault FW15D test car, equipped with passive suspension in accordance with the 1994 technical regulations, at Estoril.

the title. I'm not saying it is going to be easy, but the opportunity is there and I intend to do all I can to realize my ambition.'

Hill also confirmed that Frank Williams had told him that there would be no team orders in 1994 – unless one or other driver was firmly in the running for the Championship. He also hinted his belief that he could have won even more than three races had he not been obliged to defer to 'team orders' on a handful of occasions.

In reality, Damon's analysis could only realistically apply to the French Grand Prix – where he tailed Prost home by a fraction of a second. Monza might have been different had Prost's engine not failed and handed him victory in any case, although it is more than likely he would have been reined in at Estoril had he started from his scheduled pole position rather than from the back of the grid.

Looking back on Damon Hill's first full season with Williams, it is difficult to see that – whatever the truth of the team's strategy on the day at any individual race – he could have believed other than that he had been recruited in a supporting role to Alain Prost. Within those terms of reference, he did pretty well the perfect job.

Williams and Renault understandably centred their efforts on Alain Prost from the outset. The Frenchman finalized his agreement with the team with the specific aim of winning a fourth World Championship.

Similarly, looking forward to 1994, Ayrton Senna had joined Williams with precisely the same ambition. Damon was looking forward with relish to the challenge of measuring his own personal performance against Senna's yardstick, but the partnership was tragically pulled apart by Senna's fatal crash at Imola.

The new Williams Renault FW16 was late onto the tracks and eclipsed by the Benetton-Ford B194 of dazzling German star Michael Schumacher in the first two races of the 1994 season. At the season opener in Brazil, Damon wrestled for much of the weekend with a tiresome head cold and came away with a solid, albeit fortuitous second place. After problems in practice, he and his engineer had opted to run through the race with only the single pit stop for refuelling permitted under the new regulations, and a change of tyres. In retrospect, it was not the right strategy.

At least Hill had achieved a result. Senna spun off whilst pushing hard in Schumacher's pursuit and the Brazilian had a disappointing second round of the title chase, being spun off into a sand trap at the first corner of the Pacific Grand Prix on Japan's new TI Aida Speedway when he was pushed from behind by Mika Hakkinen's McLaren. Hill was running second to Schumacher later in the race when his transmission failed.

There was much development work to be done on the Williams FW16 before the first European race of the season, the San Marino Grand Prix at Imola. Senna qualified on pole position, but tragedy then touched Formula 1 in a manner previously only experienced on a handful of occasions in the sport's history. The Brazilian triple World Champion was killed in a fearful high speed accident whilst leading the opening stages of the race, spearing off the track at over 190mph to hit a concrete wall.

The race was restarted and Hill eventually came home a dogged sixth, despite an unscheduled pit stop to change a damaged nose cone.

Damon paid the following tribute to Senna: 'For all his concerns about safety, he never played safe in the cockpit. He performed at a hundred per cent all the time and for that he commanded admiration from every driver. I will never forget my short period working with him and consider myself immensely privileged to have been a team-mate.'

Damon Hill now had it all to do.

Bibliography

Life at the Limit, Graham Hill (William Kimber, 1969. Republished by
   Patrick Stephens Limited, 1993)
Graham, Graham Hill with Neil Ewart (Hutchinson/Stanley Paul,
   1976)
Mr Monaco, Tony Rudlin (Patrick Stephens Ltd, 1983)
Autocourse 1993/94, (Hazleton Publishing)
Autosport
Motoring News